"It's been a pleasure and a privilege to work with Charity by Design on the Best Friends bangle set. Alex and Ani understands heart disease awareness is fundamental for the health and wellbeing of all women. We would never be able to fulfill our mission without amazing partners such as Alex and Ani. We look forward to continuing and new projects with the company."

-Victoria Smith, Executive Director
American Heart Association, Founders Affiliate

"Alex and Ani is an important friend because the college and the company embrace the sustainability of resources as well as the positive values such as leadership and friendship that are associated with the charms. The college and the company are also mutually proud of our Rhode Island roots and commitment to the community."

-Dr. Nancy Carriuolo, President
Rhode Island College

"We are pleased to have Alex and Ani as sponsors of the Newport Folk and Jazz Festivals. Their first store was born in Newport and to see their growth and watch people across the nation wear their meaningful products is very special to us."

-George Wein, Founder
Newport Folk & Jazz Festivals

D1307155

Volume One, Paperback – published 2013 in the United States of America by Alex and Ani, LLC.

ISBN: 978-0-615-76112-1

Printed in the United States of America.

FOREWORD

There is a message and there is a messenger. I put this book together to show the world that you can indeed offer products that are infused with love, peace and positive energy. I also wanted to tell you about the impact of the work of a real-world leader, a woman named Carolyn Rafaelian.

- Giovanni Feroce

BLAKE AND TALITHA

"*I have a friend, Talitha. She lost her mother to brain cancer. She is a hero. She is my hero. She has a gorgeous voice that sparkles in a crowd. To sing her song, her mother's song, in front of a crowd, is braver than I could ever be. She cried. We all cried. I brought her to Alex and Ani. She deserved more than I could give her. A dolphin. For her mother. Communication, grace, strength. She is a dolphin. She is communication. She is strength. She is grace. I love her. I believe in her.*" – Blake

Talitha and Blake met while auditioning for a local production of *Oliver*!

Talitha, age nine, tells the story: "I went to try out for the role of *Oliver*. For the audition, you had to sing the song "Where is Love." I was last, so I sat there listening to kids sing the song over and over. It really made me think of my mom, and I started to get very sad. When it was my turn to sing, I cried through the whole thing, but I still acted it out, with my hands and smiles."

"Where is love? Does it fall from skies above? Is it underneath the willow tree that I've been dreaming of? Where is she who I close my eyes to see?" - From *Oliver*! Lionel Bart, 1960.

Blake, age 12, tells the story: "When Talitha came in she lit up the room. She was dressed in grey and black, with a little hat on to look like the star, *Oliver* Twist. She was proud and confident, and it made me more confident too. About nine other girls tried out before her. When it was her turn, Talitha went up, smiled, and sang, but then she lost it. She broke down, for she had recently lost her mom to brain cancer. But she kept enough confidence to finish her song. I admired her so much for having the courage to keep singing her song."

Path of Life

Carolyn Rafaelian looking out over the hills of the Israeli Judaean Desert

When thinking about your path of life, think about your plan, and every day of your life know that you're a divine gift and you're meant to have everything that your heart desires as long as your heart's desire is clear, to the point, and your vision is true to yourself.
-Carolyn

CAROLYN ON THE PATH OF LIFE

The Path of Life charm is one of Alex and Ani's most popular bracelets.

In Carolyn's words:

The three words, path of life, really resonate with people. Why? Well, we all have a path, but we hardly ever stop to question what it is. When you do, it really makes you think. Not just think, but start questioning what is meaningful to you, asking yourself, "Is where I am now where I'm supposed to be?"

I say this. We are all divinely put here for a reason, and it's what we do with our time here that matters. So when you look at those words, that symbol, *path of life*, it makes you remember that you're chosen to do this task, have this experience. But the question becomes, are you doing it the way you were intended to when you made your contract with the divine?

In my eyes, it's as if when we're placed on this earth, we come with a book, and what we record in the book is what we choose to create in our lives. Every day is a page where you create and write the story of what happened on your path of life, and what we create is up to us. We can create lightness, happiness, complaints, chaos - anything we feel like, and it all goes in the book. When you get to that last page, it's the last day of your life. You give your book back, put it back on the shelf in the grand library of books for all the world to see.

Eventually somebody comes along and starts reading it. What will they be reading? Something where they can't wait to turn the page? Or are they thinking, 'What a waste of time. Every day was a wasted day.'

You don't want to waste your days complaining, doing nothing, or not contributing on some level. Life is too precious. I value every day as a page in my book, those pages are what life is. I want my book to be so exciting that you can't wait to turn the page. I can't even wait to turn the page, when I wake up in the morning, I'm always excited to see what's next. In the end, it's the quality of the pages that matter.

How does this tie in to the path of life? How do you find your path, how do you know you're on it, and how do you create, for yourself and the world around you, an amazing and meaningful book? To me, this comes down to vision. What's your vision? Because your vision is your blueprint, and without one, it's hard to build something that makes sense. Maybe you don't know what your vision is, and thinking about that seems scary, but it's really just that you don't feel like you've hit your target yet. It's ok. Remember that every day is a new chance to write a new page, and at that point, all we have to do is take some quiet time and ask, 'What is it that I desire? What is my passion?' If you feel it's not coming to you fast enough, then say, 'Show me my passion. What is my passion?' so you can start to feel it, know it, and identify it.

Carolyn at the Church of the Holy Sepulchre Old City of Jerusalem

WHY I WEAR MY ALEX AND ANI

Alex and Ani bangles are more than just pretty jewelry; they are unique statements that speak volumes about those who wear them. They are symbols marking individual paths of life.

What follows is a collection of stories describing why people wear their Alex and Ani. The stories are personal, yet the themes are universal. We hope that in these stories you see your friends, your family, and yourself, and they inspire you as they inspired us, and lead you to ask yourself: "where am I on my path of life?"

"I stay positive because good things happen in life when I do so!"

KRISTIN

Kristin's first set of Alex and Ani bangles was an Easter gift from her mom, who bought family members matching Armenian crosses to celebrate their heritage. It's Kristin's turquoise bangle, though, that carries the most unique meaning: she bought it because she was told her grandmother's parents used to sew turquoise beads in their children's clothes in order to keep evil spirits away. Her great uncle always carried a turquoise bead in his pocket for the same reason!

Kristin was drawn to the black obsidian bangle, a Charity by Design piece designed to fundraise for the Red Cross following the 2011 Tohuku earthquake and tsunami in

Japan. She bought it to remind herself that life can take crazy, unexpected turns, and we should always support our fellow man. What Kristin didn't know at the time is that black obsidian is found in Armenia. It is known as the stone of kind-hearted and gentle people of the world and is used to block negative energy. Upon learning this information, Kristin's instinctive attraction to it made perfect sense, and the bangle is now that much more special!

"I really admire people who are not afraid of failing. I admire them even more if they are confident in their values and beliefs, mindful of their actions and have a voice."

ROSIE

After getting married in 2008, Rosie and her husband knew they wanted a family, but life was so busy. She went to graduate school. He pursued his dream career. They bought a house, did lots of renovations, and, as Rosie puts it: "We were going, going, going at a very fast pace. It was taking what seemed like a long time to start a family, and then, it happened."

Little babies, twins! Tiny faces beamed up at Rosie as she fed them, but their hands grasped earrings and pulled necklaces, and their backs got poked by bracelets and rings. Rosie thought her jewelry days were over.

She says: "Then I fell in love with Alex and Ani bangles. They rest perfectly a few inches above my wrist, so when I cuddle my boys, they never get in the way. My husband got me my first two bangles for my birthday, and little by little I am feeling more feminine. They help get me past the zombie-mommy state and make me smile every time I look at them!"

Carolyn Rafaelian's daughters, Ani and Alex

WHAT IS ALEX AND ANI

The mission at Alex and Ani is to design products that adorn the body, enlighten the mind and empower the spirit.

We are a lifestyle brand. When people wear Alex and Ani, they share the best parts of themselves with the world, revealing the highest of what has been inside them under wraps. As one Alex and Ani wearer put it, It's like "I wear my heart on my sleeve."

We hope that the women and men adorned with Alex and Ani products will feel more enlightened and empowered once they've outwardly expressed the beauty that before Alex and Ani had resided only deep within.

As Alex and Ani's product line has grown, founder and lead designer Carolyn Rafaelian has kept a deep focus on spirituality. She remains steadfast in her conviction that a person can infuse thought into material, recognizing one's power and unique essence in their everyday wear. With a deep reverence for the power of symbols, Carolyn creates adornments that do, indeed, express awareness, empowerment, and inner beauty. As she repeatedly advises, "Take the inner journey. The rewards are great." Carolyn taps into a positive energy that is deep and universal. Alex and Ani creates products that capture that energy. Then we bring them and it to the world.

"When I think of energy, I think of quiet assurance and inspired action."

DENVA

In her second year of a Ph.D program in the History of Art and Architecture at Harvard, Denva found herself struggling. She shares: "I'm here at Harvard, trying to meet expectations, and having a horrible mental running dialogue of how my intelligence measures up to other people's intelligence, wondering if this was really for me."

These negative feelings, compounded by a recent breakup, left Denva searching for a way to get grounded and gain perspective. She then hit a turning point. She shares: "I started to wake up every morning around 5:30 to work out. I found it really changed my relationship to myself and my self-worth – it gave me something to really bring my energy to."

Denva's roommate Melissa gave her an Alex and Ani bangle with a single gemstone: the sodalite. Sodalite is the stone of the athlete, and one of its properties is self-assurance. For Denva, the gift was significant on many levels.

She notes: "Just by this gift, my roommate was acknowledging how much my self-perception had radically changed through the process of physical exertion, moving my body, trusting my body, and trusting my emotions. Once you get re-centered into your body and move it, you begin to trust that awareness. Your sadness is real, but there are other things that you can do to re-funnel that energy. So the gift meant so much to me – it is a wonderful touchstone to have, it shows the commitment I made to myself."

From the Beginning

FROM THE BEGINNING: THE HISTORY OF ALEX AND ANI

As a child, Carolyn spent plenty of time at Cinerama, her father Ralph Rafaelian's jewelry factory in Cranston, Rhode Island. As a young adult, Carolyn experimented with other career paths, but in the end, she always came back to design. After college, she returned to her roots and began working out of Cinerama, side by side with her father and sister, Rebecca, and later, her niece, Rachel. Ralph worked primarily in rhinestones, but Carolyn experimented with different materials and fabrications that she sold to mainstream retailers, though in the end, that really wasn't her passion.

As she puts it: "I was designing for commercial outlets that were very much like 'OK, well now we're working with this color palette, or with this silhouette,' and I just wanted to do my own thing, stuff that I would actually wear. That's when Alex and Ani was created."

The early Alex and Ani designs were big, chunky pieces. Eventually, Carolyn found that what she really loved were the symbolic pieces that she liked to give as gifts, like a bangle with St. Christopher (the patron saint of travelers) for someone who was going away and needed protection. As Carolyn describes it: "I'd see people and they'd still have the bracelet I gave them on; they'd tell me how much it meant to them and how they never took it off and I'm like, that's what it's all about. So I just kept being true to who I am and next thing you know the business became a business, just by being me staying true, organically."

The fact that people love the substance behind Alex and Ani pieces is important to Carolyn. Those who wear Alex and Ani look to their personal collections for inspiration, to remind them of important events, to tell their stories, to channel their power. These sentiments breathe life into the essence of what Carolyn's creations are all about. She shares: "As things grew, I realized that we all feel a certain level of connection with different people, things, situations, memories … jewelry is a medium to represent connections … I mean, you don't hear people say 'Oh I wear this t-shirt every day because my grandmother gave it to me.' You wear this ring, this necklace, this bracelet; it's something that you can wear every day and be reminded of what's important to you."

"Externally, anything can be pretty, without substance, it's just that. When you add that layer of substance in it, it becomes strength: strong and purposeful."

Carolyn and Rebecca Rafaelian with family

Ralph Rafaelian

The original Cinerama factory in Cranston, RI

RALPH RAFAELIAN (1935-2012)

At Alex and Ani, jewelry making runs in the family. Carolyn's father, Ralph Rafaelian, was a self-made entrepreneur who designed and manufactured jewelry in Rhode Island for decades. Ralph was born in 1935 in Providence. His father, Melkon Rafaelian, emigrated from Mush, Turkey to the United States in 1915, just before the Armenian genocide that killed over 1.5 million people, including every single member of Melkon's family.

A few years later, Melkon met Ralph's mother, Mariam, in France where she and her sisters had fled from Armenia to escape the genocide. Melkon and Mariam married in 1927, and returned to Rhode Island where they had four children: Lillian, Virginia, Anna, and Ralph. Mariam died of cancer at the age of 44, and Melkon went on to raise his children alone. He finally remarried in 1959.

Ralph was an insightful and thoughtful man who seemed surprised at what he was able to accomplish in building Cinerama, his jewelry business. His desk at the Alex and Ani manufacturing building was piled high with papers, pictures, and small boxes of his beloved rhinestone creations. He was an insightful, humble man, and while leaning back in his chair he described his modest beginnings with pride. Ralph made it clear that he never forgot where he came from or what it felt like to be the odd man out. He shared: "I've been poor. We grew up in a very unprivileged situation in East Providence – my neighbors were Gypsies, Blacks, we were all considered second-class citizens. My parents were immigrants, they didn't speak English very well, but we had ambition, and have done really well."

Carolyn and her father, Ralph Rafaelian at the Cinerama manufacturing facility

After finishing high school, Ralph was drafted, and served his country on a naval destroyer escort for two years. Upon returning home, he worked as an assistant trainee at a McLellan five-and-dime store. Even then, Ralph's ideas for improving systems brewed: "I worked at McLellan for six months. I wasn't learning anything from the manager; the things I wanted to do to innovate the business were deemed unacceptable. One day, I was downstairs talking with the man who took the cardboard from the business. When he found out that I was Armenian, he asked, 'what are you doing working for somebody else?' Not that all Armenians work for themselves, but it was just something that stuck in my mind." Ultimately, Ralph's desire for greater autonomy led him to leave McLellan and work for his brother-in-law in the jewelry business.

This was the late 1950's, and the jewelry business in Rhode Island was booming, employing thousands and thousands of people. It was an easy business to get into, as Ralph put it, "you just got one room with low rent, and made jewelry, it was very simple to do." Ralph worked for his brother-in-law for six years, running manufacturing and doing some designing. The standard distribution chain for jewelry then was from manufacturer to wholesaler, to retailer to customer. However, as Ralph explained: "I've always been ambitious – I wanted to achieve. I had the idea of selling directly to organizations, which turned out to be real productive. I started selling a rhinestone American flag pin to Daughters of the American Revolution as a fundraising item. The Vietnam War had just started so people were looking to wear something patriotic. I made $5,000 for the company, without interfering with my regular work, but at the end of the year they gave me only a small bonus. It was very low compared to others in the industry. So that's when I decided,

if I can do it for them, I can do it for myself, and I started my own business."

In 1965, Ralph opened a little room on Empire Street in downtown Providence. There, he made his flag pins: he set them up, soldered them, had them plated and shipped directly to fundraising organizations. His concept caught on almost immediately, and he started selling patriotic jewelry to organizations like the Veterans of Foreign Wars. As he puts it: "My expenses were very low: I hired high school kids from a local Catholic school; I got about five or six girls from there and then they brought their friends in, so I had about ten girls from Fox Point working for me, and they were phenomenal, probably the best crew I ever had. I was making one item, the rhinestone flag pin, and later I made red, white and blue earrings, things to match it."

Ralph's business expanded rapidly – a year later he bought a building on Providence's Eddy Street, and two years after that, a 12,000 square foot building in nearby Cranston, Rhode Island. He continued to do very well in jewelry design, manufacturing and wholesaling. Eventually, Carolyn began to work in the family trade, first designing costume jewelry for retail outlets, and later, by patenting the expandable bangle concept. It was from there that Alex and Ani was born: a company that would eventually take over some space in Ralph's business, Cinerama, a place where many original Cinerama workers remain.

Ralph recalled: "About 10 years ago Carolyn joined the business; my daughter Rebecca had been with me longer, since right after college, she knows the manufacturing quite well. The business kept growing, but these past few years Carolyn's products have just exploded. It just evolved. We are one of the few companies left that are still manufacturing

Ralph Rafaelian at a trade show and his trademark rhinestone American flag pin

a product. If you see any of the other jewelry companies out there, they're not manufacturing – they're importing from China. They're re-carding it over here, to make it look American-made, and that's basically it, but as for actual manufacturers, there are very few."

Ralph took great pride in keeping the Rhode Island jewelry industry alive by employing a significant number of people. "Besides manufacturing in-house, we keep one plater totally busy delivering three times a week, they probably employ 10-15 people. We have a wiring house that does work for us, as well as stamping people, so our work touches many people."

Ralph defined success as "starting something from nothing and making it grow," but he was quick to include that true success includes the spirit of generosity. He takes great pride in

Alex and Ani's philanthropic contributions, as well as their Charity by Design work. Ralph was most proud of the role his company has played over the years in the local economy: the jobs it created, and the livings made by his workforce. He kept a watchful eye over Carolyn as Alex and Ani grew to new heights, while keeping in step with his philosophies of generosity, local production and good works. He admitted a certain awe with this transformation, as he says: "Carolyn has taken it to a level I'd never dreamed of." Ralph Rafaelian was a beloved husband, father and champion for those less fortunate. His legacy continues at Alex and Ani and Cinerama alike.

"For me, I just look at things, not as good, not as bad, or anything like that. I see it simply as the experience of what it was, and how I got to challenge and shape that experience. Ultimately, I see how my perspective changed the outcome to what worked for me, because I had the power to do so. I own that power to do so, and I'm here to tell people that you have the same power. You have to acknowledge that you DO have that power. It's not made up, it's as real as it gets. Once you really get this simple, fundamental thing that it's all in your perspective, it changes everything."

- Carolyn

REBECCA

Rebecca was thrilled to discover Alex and Ani because she's always on the lookout for tokens that inspire her to act. In her bangles, she finds something wearable, artful, and functional. She describes her Path of Life charm as a guide for her will; a reminder to stay grounded, not be too spontaneous, but also, to take risks.

As she describes it: "The Path of Life charm is a reminder that sometimes, getting to where you're going is messy. You just have to be ok with it, it's all part of the path."

Rebecca also wears the Star of Venus. Initially, she was drawn to it because it reminded her of the daisy that was on everything from her wedding cake to her wedding invitations. She was shocked and thrilled to learn the image was actually one that represented love and affection -- a perfect symbol for the deep love she feels for her husband and two-year-old son.

"My greatest gift is my insatiable need to learn something new."

BRENDON

Brendon loves the water, so it's fitting that he discovered Alex and Ani in Newport, Rhode Island, while marveling at sailboats, dreaming of owning one. He stumbled on the Alex and Ani store, and instead bought a sailboat bangle, thus starting his collection. His second bangle was an anchor, a gift from his love, representing stability, strength, and being in a solid and anchored relationship.

"I also wear the oyster, because it's a beauty that you don't see right away. The exterior isn't too pretty, but when you open it, it's beautiful. I think you should look at a lot of things like that in life. Sometimes you don't see the best exterior, but you just have to look inside to find something beautiful to pull out."

"When I think of energy I think of an entity that possesses the power to initiate a positive change."

"I feel most relaxed and happy when I'm at home with my twin sister and our three fur babies -- particularly if it's a beautiful morning and we can sit outside and have a nice cup of coffee and hear nature singing."

MEG AND MARIE

Twin sisters Meg and Marie love their Alex and Ani. To them, the bangles personify their optimistic outlooks on life and remind them of the importance of family and friends.

Meg wears hers to promote positive feelings and attitudes, and her favorite charm is the four leaf clover. It reminds her that when you're feeling negative, there is indeed something positive out there. "You just have to uncover it, just as you have to uncover a four leaf clover."

She says: "I wear my Alex and Ani to work every day to remind me that all I have to do is be positive and the luck will follow. Now I share the bangles with my family and friends so I can widen the positivism circle!"

Marie loves the Tree of Life bangle. She looks to it as a symbol for staying grounded. She believes a tree is only as sturdy as the roots underneath it; in order to be strong, she strives to maintain deep roots. Marie believes in the power of positive energy, saying that energy is a gift that not only radiates goodness, but can also neutralize someone else's negativity. She also believes in faith, hope and strength, and that the lessons you learn in bad situations will carry you toward better things on the path ahead.

JENN

After losing her mother Merle to Breast Cancer years ago, Jenn finds solace in Breast Cancer awareness tokens. Still struggling with a deep sense of loss 17 years later, she was seeking a particularly meaningful way to honor and remember her mother. Stumbling on the "M" bangle at Alex and Ani, Jenn was reminded of her young daughters, Madison and Morgan, whose energy perfectly reflects her mother's spirit and warmth. Now, she looks at her arm and sees M: Merle, Madison, and Morgan. For Jenn, it's a token of love and everlasting connectedness.

"I also bought a heart, which reminds me that my mother is always in my heart...so when I am sad, I can look down and smile. I love these bracelets, and having a reason to buy them makes them even more special to me."

"I stay positive because I realize how very fortunate I am to have a wonderful life, as crazy as it is at times."

KELLY

Kelly is a middle school teacher at a small charter school in Central Falls, Rhode Island.

The work is constant, but she loves her job, and seeing the impact she has on her students' lives makes it all worthwhile. Kelly sees her bright collection of beaded Alex and Ani bangles as a reminder to let her bubbly personality shine through in the classroom, and to create a safe and encouraging environment where her students can thrive.

"I am most influenced by my students. They make me work harder each day than I ever thought I could, and all I want to do is continue learning and providing them with great opportunities to rise. I love my Alex and Ani, and wearing them each day represents the determined, strong, and dynamic teacher, role model, and caring person I have grown up to be."

"I really admire someone who does 'whatever it takes' to succeed, whether this be in their career, the classroom, or any other situation where they do not give up and keep persevering."

(+) ENERGY = POSITIVE ENERGY

The mission at Alex and Ani is to spread positive energy, which is something that Carolyn and the entire Alex and Ani family take very seriously.

In Carolyn's words:
"Positive attracts positive: that's science, but positive also attracts negative. Anything with power needs charging to survive, when that power depletes, the search begins to find more. It's the same thing with human nature, or anything living for that matter. There is a constant need to find more power, whether that's activating power within, or seeking an external source. If someone finds power they're going to be drawn towards it."

She continues: "When God said we're all created equal, my interpretation of that is we all inherently have the gift to elevate, and to ascend. Those who need elevation will find themselves among people they can emulate because they need to be in that energy field, to pull in some of that energy for themselves."

This might seem intimidating. You might wonder, 'if someone approached me with negative energy, will they drain me? If they're attracted to my ability to ascend, will they just pull me down?' The answer is yes, they can, but … they don't have to. As Carolyn puts it, it's all about perception, and all people inherently have the power, through their perceptions, to control situations that might otherwise feel overwhelming.

She notes: "When you find you're in a situation that doesn't feel right to you, just listen to that feeling, because it is saying everything to you. Use your power, ask yourself, 'why does this person make me feel like I don't want to be here right now? Then say, I'm here to learn something from this experience; what could it possibly be?' At the end of all this, know that the divine is always working on your behalf to give you the experiences that you need in order to grow. Some of it may seem so unpleasant that you wonder, why did I have to go through that? But realize the experience put you in a different direction - maybe emotionally, maybe physically, maybe mentally, but it's the direction you needed to be in. Look at a negative thing as an adjustment, because it's nothing more than that. It's an opportunity to say to yourself, I'm going to take this experience and let it mold me into the greater shape that I need to be so I can really follow my life's path."

"My favorite thing about these charms is that I get to decide how to wear them. They can help to promote personal strength, remind me to stay calm, or tell me I'm pretty when no one else may."

JENNIFER

Five years ago, Jennifer started an intensive teacher training program in Pilates. What happened in the process was a mental and spiritual opening that Jennifer was completely unprepared for. She realized that she had been beating herself up for years, and when faced with this reality, she had no idea how to respond to or cope with it. Jennifer had to learn how to purge the negative, and forgive herself for the past, so she started wearing Alex and Ani as little reminders to do so.

Jennifer loves that Alex and Ani bangles are expandable. She compares that expandability to the way energy can expand and contract individuals. She notes the way the body might respond to emotional situations as an example:

"Say you're in a very serious relationship that suddenly ends. Heartbreak sets in and along with puffy eyes, your body becomes hunched in a fetal-like position. Shoulders forward, chin down. Most people suffering from heartbreak share this posture, but after a while the heartbreak goes away and you move on. In some cases though, the muscle memory of that event does not go away, resulting in back, shoulder and neck pain. The body protects us physically from emotional pain. The body doesn't lie, but the mind does, creating

stories of judgment, negativity, and conflict leaving our bodies with no choice but to absorb that toxicity. Haven't you ever been with someone who is in a grumpy mood and said, 'Wow, you're in a bad mood!'? What most do not realize is that just by making that statement, that person's grumpy energy has already rubbed off on you, therefore putting you in a bad mood even if only for a second. Thankfully, positivity works the same way." In Jennifer's path to healing, she sees the expansion of positivity as a key element in her quest to change.

"When I purchase a new bracelet I have to put it on and take it off a few times to break it in until eventually, it fits me perfectly. These bangles can act as a sugar pill; a trick stimulant that helps keep my ego, esteem, and state of mind in check. Putting them on is my way of settling my own demons. I believe that I infuse these bangles with my energy, good or bad, and wearing them reminds me of that choice, good or bad - I make my own energy. I'm not physically taking a pill, but I am physically putting a bangle on. It's the act of doing something for myself to help stay positive. I can expand, contract or meditate with them. I love the charms and all the adornments, but it is the bracelet's design itself that keeps me most centered."

SHIRLEY

When Shirley and her husband separated, she found herself in emotional turmoil. As she began her healing process, she discovered Alex and Ani. She shares: "Alex and Ani touched me because I believe that words are power, and what people put out into the world comes back to them, so I immediately felt a connection."

Shirley started her collection with the green birthstone bangle to honor her son, whose attitude toward life is a source of constant inspiration. She admires him for being well-rounded and willing to experience new cultures and new things, traits that remind her to keep learning, and not get stuck. Since then, Shirley has collected bangles to represent where she is on her new journey.

She continues: "I love knowing that I am wearing my journey on my arm, and at any time can look at one of my bangles and recall where I was at that time in my life. Thank you Alex and Ani, because now I can really wear my heart on my sleeve."

"When I think of energy I think of a positive feeling that comes from within, or that surrounds you when you are near people with positive energy."

DENILLE

"Why I wear my Alex and Ani ... that is what everyone asks me. Everyone wants to know what they mean to me. It started out as a fun obsession, but when I saw the owl charm, tears came to my eyes. After my very loved grandfather passed away, my aunt started hearing an owl hoot outside her home. Soon after, my mother started hearing one as well. It's been said that an owl is a reincarnation of someone you've been close to. I do not know if that is true or not, but anytime I hear an owl I smile and think of my grandfather in his happy and healthy days. Recently, I was walking my dog and saw an owl swoop down in front of me and I thought, 'Oh! That's Pepe.'"

Denille loves the words Alex and Ani associate with her owl charm; she feels they personify her grandfather. As she says: "Wisdom, because he was the wise man in the family – the person every-one looked up to; protection, because he was the protector of the family and took great care of my grandmother; and transition, because we now have to get used to life without him."

"Vibrancy is a ray of light, somebody's being, beauty and love on the inside. Somebody's energy really makes them vibrant."

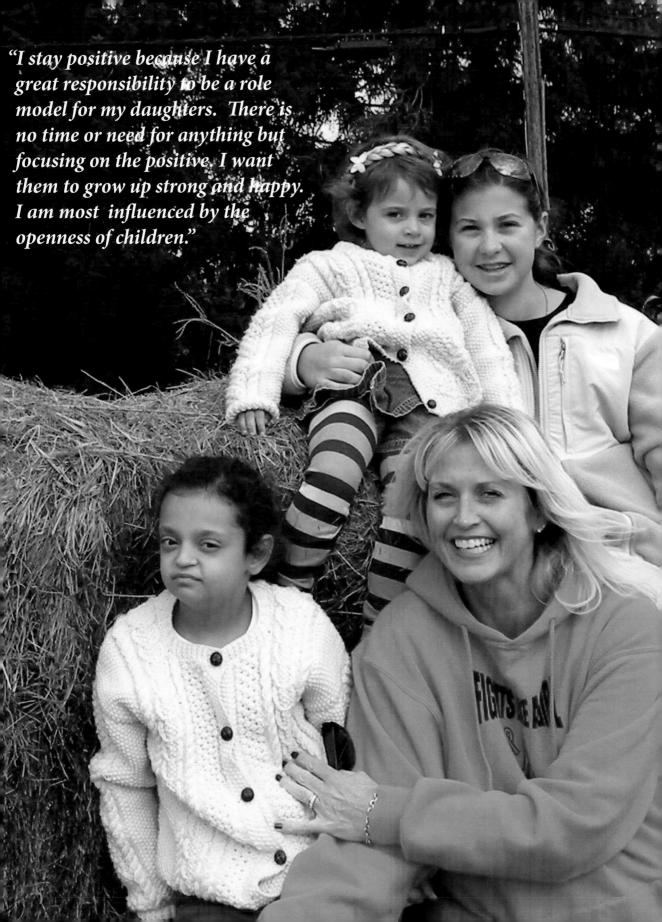

"I stay positive because I have a great responsibility to be a role model for my daughters. There is no time or need for anything but focusing on the positive. I want them to grow up strong and happy. I am most influenced by the openness of children."

KERRY

"I have three beautiful daughters ages twelve, nine, and three. My middle daughter has special needs; a rare chromosomal abnormality. Needless to say, it has been nine years of an absolute emotional roller coaster ride. The Alex and Ani bangle I have says "laugh." Keeping a great sense of humor and a positive attitude has brought her far and helped our family. I look at my bangle and it reminds and inspires me to keep on laughing!"

Made in America, With Love

CAROLYN ON MADE IN AMERICA AND WHAT IT MEANS FOR ENERGY

At the core of Carolyn's philosophy lies something very simple, and it's what drives the vision and practices of the company: spreading positive energy. Central to this mission is Carolyn's capacity to closely control the process by which her products are made: the manufacturing environment at Alex and Ani, where the raw materials used originate, and what's in them.

As Carolyn explains it: "Jewelry has an energy; it's conductive. So for any piece, who it's created by, where it's created, and the synergies achieved in that process wind up in the DNA of that piece: it creates an energy. If you don't know who is making what you wear, what kind of labor conditions it was produced in, or what kinds of toxins are in the metals, it does nothing to elevate your vibration, but it does everything to keep it low. In contrast, if you're aware of these things, what the piece was born into, its intention, you increase your own energy through its integrity. Everything that I am as a person is in my product. It's coming from a sacrosanct place that I hold as my personal truth. By controlling my production I know who's making my product, and how it's made, and in doing that, I set positive energy into motion."

Crucial to Carolyn's philosophy is that all Alex and Ani products are sourced, designed, and manufactured in the United States.

As Carolyn describes it: "It's important to me, 'made in America.' My goal in life, as long as I'm here, is to protect this place. My story is an illustration of what's great about it, what's magic about it. This is a country where freedom is valued. I don't want outsourcing to tarnish what we've worked to solidify the roots of what this country's all about. Because when you take the roots out you start killing the foundation, and that leaves weakness. Wherever there's weakness, destruction follows, which leaves no room for ascendance. So I need to keep those roots intact and nourished, and that's my duty with an American made product."

Giovanni Feroce
CEO/Alex and Ani

Bryant University
World Trade Day

"There was a time when the term 'Made in America' was synonymous with quality, innovation, and an overall commitment to excellence. And there were many who said it never could return. Made in America is a promise of quality once again, it's a statement to be uttered with pride once again, and so too, is made in Rhode Island."

Raw materials in manufacturing

MANUFACTURING ALEX AND ANI

Rebecca Rafaelian has worked in the jewelry business her entire life, beginning with her dad's company, Cinerama, which she now co-owns and operates as an exclusive Alex and Ani manufacturer. She recalls days growing up when her mom would send her, along with big sister Carolyn, out to the Cinerama factory to work. They'd do small tasks like bagging jewelry or putting it on cards, learning the trade from the ground up as their father intended.

As she got older, Rebecca devoted more and more time to the factory, and her responsibilities increased to supervising, ordering, and fostering the relationships created by her dad with subcontractors and vendors. When Rebecca graduated from the University of Rhode Island with a degree in business in 1990, it was clear she'd make a career out of running the manufacturing side of the family business. As she puts it: "It's been full force ever since."

Things have changed since 1990, and what started out as running the Cinerama factory has shifted to running Alex and Ani's. As Rebecca tells it: "The biggest change was the conscious decision we made to dedicate the factory to the growth of Alex and Ani. For years, we exclusively did business as wholesalers, but as Carolyn was building Alex and Ani, it became evident that we needed to focus on her brand and help develop it fully."

Craftsmanship at the Cinerama manufacturing facility

When asked what she thinks about the growth and popularity of Alex and Ani, she replies: "It's mind blowing. For years we always thought, it's coming, it's coming, stick with it. You look back and it seems like it took so long, but it's amazing to see how the whole thing evolved, and where we are now. It's cool, it's crazy. If people think it was an overnight thing, then they don't know what went into it on the back end, because for years, it was us sitting in a tiny room with an accountant and my dad being like, what are we doing?"

Rebecca notes that in the end, Carolyn wanted "to be her own person, bring her own thing, and not worry about what other stores wanted." So they persevered, and through the strength of hanging together and staying true to their vision, success arrived.

Walk onto the manufacturing floor at Alex and Ani and you'll immediately realize that this is no processing plant. Natural light streams through large windows onto a wide and airy work area. Piles of sparkling beads, gleaming wire and hand tools dot the work stations where employees, some of whom have been with the company since the 1980's, do their handiwork.

As Rebecca describes it: "It's very warm, not a factory-like environment. We have, thanks to Carolyn, art deco lighting, oriental rugs, and hardwood floors. It's a very nice atmosphere, as opposed to our competitors where it's literally like a factory: cinderblock walls, and no windows."

In addition to providing a warm and aesthetically pleasing work environment, Alex and Ani is highly aware of their individual responsibility to nurture, love, and preserve the environment. All materials used in Alex and Ani products are made in America, and are of recycled or sustainable metals. Additionally, suppliers to Alex and Ani practice eco-conscious habits that support the mission and values of the company.

"The Workbench" where Carolyn Rafaelian and her father would collaborate on design

"I am most influenced by my stepdad. He taught me the glass is always half full, never half empty, and whenever you get the chance, dance. He taught me to live life to the fullest."

KIM

Kim describes her Alex and Ani as: "little circles of her life" or "chapters of her book", right there on her wrist. She has charms that signify important aspects of her life: her wedding, the initial of her husband's first name, and a four leaf clover to remind her how lucky she is. Kim wears a variety of black and silver beads to remind her that nothing in life is black and white, but mostly shades of gray, and in order to be happy in life, you must keep an open mind.

Finally, Kim wears an Om bangle, which acts as a root connection for her, so much that she once took her's off her wrist and gave it to her

mom, whom she so admires.

"My Alex and Ani … they have become my good luck charms, my worry stones, my peace of mind. I wear eight right now that I never take off. When I hear the little jingle of my charms, I smile. When I get stressed from everyday life situations, I hold them and remember what I am so thankful for."

KATIE

Katie wears her Alex and Ani as a tribute to her late mentor, boss, and friend, Cyndi. From Cyndi, Katie learned what she calls her greatest lessons: how to approach life, and how to approach death. Katie admired that though facing an end-of-life illness, Cyndi kept a smile on her face and encouraged those around her to laugh and enjoy life along with her. Rather than fear the sunset of her life, she implored others to embrace every moment leading up to it with laughter, joy and smiles. Now, when faced with tough situations, Katie realizes that happiness is about how you look at things, and how you choose to approach adversity. Through Cyndi's influence, Katie has found the power to remain happy and positive.

"Cyndi was a woman of so many talents, and her personal philosophy in life taught me so much. I wear the October birthstone, the breast cancer awareness charm, and the "live" and "peace" bangles in her honor. They're simple reminders to live the way she did."

"I stay positive because a great woman once told me to 'pull up my big girl panties and deal with it' so face life with a smile and love the ones you are with."

VICTORIA

Victoria is not a big jewelry person; she only wears pieces that have a special meaning to her. She is enchanted by Alex and Ani bangles, loving that each piece not only has its own meaning, but also a meaning to her personally.

Victoria was drawn to the owl. The owl represents wisdom and protection, but to Victoria, it reminds her of a trip to Barcelona where she and her friends stayed near a building topped with a giant owl sculpture. Whenever they felt lost, they'd spot the owl high in the air and use it as a compass to find their way home. For Victoria, the owl on her wrist is a constant reminder that transition and change is part of life, but in your heart, you can always find your way home.

"I really admire someone who follows their dreams and does what they love to do, regardless of what it takes them to get there, while balancing all aspects of their life. I also really admire someone who goes out of their way to make a real connection with someone or help others."

"*I am most influenced by our dreams and our drive to accomplish goals. I want to make sure that we get to do all we want to do in life, and never feel like we've wasted time.*"

ADAM AND CASEY

Adam and Casey met a few years ago through a mutual friend, just as Adam had joined the Army and was headed to boot camp. The two stayed in touch, and over time their relationship evolved into the truest of love. They discussed marriage, and shortly after Adam proposed, he was deployed to Iraq. Adam and Casey married before he left, and Casey's hectic and uncertain life as an Army wife began.

Casey was introduced to Alex and Ani with a Star of David Bangle, a gift from her best friend. Now, Casey has a little collection, but her favorite is the Path of Life charm, because it helps her get through the worst of Army life.

Casey explains that it's tough to deal with Adam's training and deployments, but the hardest part is preparing for whatever the Army decides they need to do next, having no idea what that might be. She says, "You're always preparing yourself for what's coming next, wondering if we're actually going to do it, or if it's going to fall through." Casey says it's in these times that she looks to her Path of Life charm to remind her that, "Regardless of what's going on, as mixed up as everything gets, I'm still moving towards something."

Carolyn Rafaelian in some of her signature designs

SUCCESS IS BEING COMFORTABLE IN YOUR OWN SKIN

In Carolyn's words:

"The biggest compliment I ever received was, 'You are so comfortable being you.' I guess this must be a gift, because it never dawned on me to be anything otherwise, and I was surprised to find that not everyone has that same feeling. Personally, I acknowledge my greatness, but my greatness is not an exception - it's the norm. See, everybody has it, but not everybody realizes it, and that's the difference.

How comfortable are you in your own skin, playing your role in this life? Do you have a solid foundation? If you don't, then some insecurities are going to feel very exposed … perhaps just on the surface, but they have deep roots.

It's our responsibility to overcome insecurities or doubts that we put upon ourselves because they're just veils. They're not real, they're illusions that we hold as truth. Because when you come to your core, the essence of your being, who are you really? Are you your chubby body? Or are you, for example, the teacher that was put here to nurture young people, to put them on their life's path?

In life, you need to ask yourself: 'am I an asset to mankind, or am I a liability?' If you're playing the role of being a liability, you're not servicing anyone, but worse, you're not servicing yourself. Ask how you're affecting everything, and how can you affect it on a bigger scale? What's your power? How fabulous can you make your character, and how can you positively influence the characters around you?

Remember this. When you strip yourself of a body, you're left with an essence: you are a form of energy. Right now, you are a light being condensed in this body, a vehicle that lets you travel through life. Some vehicles are fast, some are beautiful, some have dents, some need work, whatever. The purpose of this vehicle is to help navigate your life as you engage in life experiences – and life is a journey."

SHAWN

Shawn finds that sometimes, her life can get very stressful.

"I work too much ... I stress too much ... my commute is too long ... I don't exercise enough ... my life gets WAY out of balance." Shawn had some Alex and Ani bangles that she thought were fun and fashionable, but it wasn't until a long summer break on Martha's Vineyard that she started looking at them as tangible reminders of a newly set goal. She says "I spent that summer consciously working toward balance and positivity, trying to put priority on the important things in my life.

I bought the dolphin charm because I've always loved dolphins, but additionally, it's really meaningful. It's a symbol that represents making time for play, communication, and joyfulness. It's a reminder to take things lightly. I also wear the clear stone for clarity and simplicity. It reminds me to un-complicate things .... it's a conscious decision."

"I stay positive because positivity leads to openness, and openness leads to wonderful opportunities."

CHRISTEN

Christen loves her Alex and Ani, and she wears her bangles daily as a testament to her personal growth in times of transition. "I wear the feather because to me, it symbolizes growth and represents the changes that happen in life. A feather constantly floats and moves through space, lightly transitioning from one place to another. When I look at my feather I am reminded to grow, to find truth, and to reach new levels in my career and in my life.

I also wear the pearl in the shell. The pearl is my birthstone. My pastor once said that in order for a pearl to form, it has to go through a process, to travel through the digestive tract of the oyster to develop, grow, becoming unique and beautiful. To me, the pearl is a representation of something beautiful at the end of a long process, the end result of a struggle. The pearl I wear on my wrist represents the person I am now.

I stay positive because I believe that you get back what you put out. When I feel and act positive, it's returned to me."

"I really admire someone who is living out their dreams and their destiny."

WHAT IS THE POWER OF ONE?

The Power of One is a transfer of energy, love and positivity. It's a gesture of admiration - an acknowledgment and affirmation of the light in all of us.

The Power of One is a spontaneous event, it can happen in the act of comforting, reminiscing, protecting, healing, laughing, or joyfully enchanting!

Once, while with a friend in the drive through line at the bank, Carolyn looked over and spotted a woman singing so passionately in her car that her energy was bursting through the windows. Instantly, Carolyn took off a bangle and said, "Allison, give her this and tell her how much we love her!"

Allison rolled down the window and motioned to get the woman's attention, who, of course, was completely embarrassed. Carolyn and Allison yelled, "No! We love you! We want to give you this!"

The woman was floored by the gesture. According to Carolyn, "It was as if we had given her a bar of gold. She had that whole, unbelievable, overwhelmed emotion you get when you realize that another human being is, number one, being kind; and number two, acknowledging your uniqueness. It's called the Power of One. And you do it 'cause it's from your heart."

Two friends exchange an Alex and Ani bangle

I'M PUTTING THIS ON YOU WITH THE INTENTION OF LOVE

In Carolyn's words:

"Whenever you have an interaction with somebody, it's an exchange of energy: thought, form or motion. When you interact with an *intention*, it's different, you're making a deliberate effort to call in that energy. Putting something like a bracelet, or even a jacket, on someone with an *intention* instantly creates a synergy between the recipient and the person holding the intention.

When you verbalize 'I put this on you with the intention of love,' you call that energy in, and that love now circulates around the piece. You're saying, *as I put this piece around you, I'm whispering into it my intention that you are surrounded by love*, and the piece now becomes a sort of protective shield. By doing this, you have put something into motion. You made a specific prayer, specifically identifying the energy to do something. By doing an act with intention, you create energy, passing it to someone so it becomes exposed around them."

Carolyn puts an expandable love bracelet on a friend

SARAH

Sarah was introduced to Alex and Ani by an unlikely close friend - her husband's ex-wife. The more she learned about Alex and Ani bangles, the more she loved them! Sarah hit a particularly rough patch last year, and was looking for daily reminders to be positive. Her growing Alex and Ani collection served that purpose well. Sarah's favorite bangle is her starfish charm. To her, the starfish is a symbol of regeneration, reminding her that if life chops her off at the leg, she can and will grow a new one. An affirming reminder indeed.

Sarah has discovered the pleasure of the "Power of One," giving someone an Alex and Ani bangle straight from her wrist. Not long ago, a close friend who'd just lost a brother asked Sarah if the world would ever be less dark than it was at that moment. Sarah snapped her Laugh bangle off of her wrist and affirmed: "Yes it will. Put this on, and remember things will brighten up."

"I look forward to earning my laugh lines. When you smile every day, it wears a path on your face. What an incredible badge of honor to have, being able to show the world that you've spent your days in laughter."

MEGAN

Megan has an enlarged heart, a condition that often left her worried and reluctant to plan for the future. One afternoon, after a particularly stressful doctor appointment, Megan and a girlfriend visited the Alex and Ani Boston store. There she was drawn to the Path of Life bangle, which she purchased for strength, motivation, and energy – exactly what she needed that afternoon! As she puts it: "The charm helps me remember that everything is what you make it – life's existence is more about your spirit and your energy, and less about the body's physical canvas."

"My greatest gift is my heart, literally and metaphorically. My heart has never given up the fight or journey of the life I want to experience and it is the reason I love so hard in the present moment each and every day."

"I love my Alex and Ani bangles because for me, it symbolizes my fight, my victory!"

KARA

In a routine physical following the birth of her son, Kara found out she had breast cancer. For Kara, who felt fine, the news was a total shock. She was told she'd need immediate treatment, including intense radiation and chemotherapy. Her family and friends rallied around her.

Kara's sister-in-law gave her two Alex and Ani bangles: a four leaf clover, and a green gemstone charm, to keep with the "luck of the Irish" theme. Kara later purchased the pink birthstone bangle, wearing it to her treatments as a symbol of strength and courage.

Every time she'd see it sparkle, Kara was reminded to keep going, that, as she puts it, "life is too short to sweat the small stuff."

Kara says: "I've always been on the quiet side, but I think having been through all of this I'm a better advocate for myself, so I really admire someone who can speak up for what they believe in and what is right."

SARAH

Sarah is an opera singer who, after recently finishing a master's degree at The Boston Conservatory, now lives in New York City. She wears her Alex and Ani every day because they give her strength and energy, and make her feel inspired to do great things! More than once, people have stopped her on the street to ask where she got them, or pulled up their sleeves to reveal their own collection. Sarah finds wearing Alex and Ani a remarkable way to meet a stranger and share a special connection.

Last spring, Sara starred in an off-Broadway production of The Mikado, an opera based on Japanese life. While the show was running, Japan was hit by the devastating 2011 Tohoku earthquake and tsunami. Sara gave the show's

director and choreographer the Alex and Ani Obsidian bangle, a piece designed by Carolyn Rafaelian to support the Japan relief efforts. Sara says, "The director and choreographer loved and appreciated the bangles, and pretty soon the whole cast bought them in support of the cause. It was really exciting." Sara loves the momentum and energy this gesture created: the cast and crew rallied to provide support for those hit by that tragic event.

Charity by Design Vice President Nicki Castonguay-Maher and Carolyn Rafaealian

CHARITY
— BY —
DESIGN

At the heart of Alex and Ani is the most powerful of all positive energies, love. Our passion for making the dreams of charitable organizations come true is channeled through Charity by Design, a unique department focused solely upon giving. Charity by Design empowers non-profit organizations to reach their goals by sharing what we do best, the power of positive energy through innovative, creative design. Our customized symbolic charms capture the essence of a charity, making it more accessible to the public while raising awareness and funds. Proceeds are donated directly to non-profit organizations who strive to enhance the quality of lives, or life, on earth.

I AM A HASBRO CHILDREN'S HOSPITAL HERO

The Charity by Design Hero bangle launched in May of 2011 and remains one of Alex and Ani's most popular pieces to date. Funds raised from the sale of the Hero bangle support programs, research, and the training of doctors and caregivers at the Rhode Island-based Hasbro Children's Hospital: a place of healing that brings world-class experts, the latest technology, and innovative research together to address the common and uncommon health needs of children.

The hospital's Pediatrician-in-Chief and Medical Director, Dr. Robert Klein, is an enthusiastic supporter of the Hero bangle. He loves the fact that a Rhode Island-based company came up with such a creative and community-based way to support the amazing heroes who walk the hospital's halls on a daily basis. He says: "We are proud of what we do, and of the amazing numbers of heroes in this hospital. The patients, families, the caregivers – they are brave, diligent and caring."

Dr. Klein calls the Hero bangle "a spectacular effort that is much more than a fundraiser. It's an emblem that represents the dedication and innovation of the entire Hasbro Children's Hospital family, and the community that supports it."

MAYOR'S ALLIANCE FOR NYC'S ANIMALS

The Mayor's Alliance for NYC's Animals is a coalition of over 150 animal rescue groups and shelters working with Animal Care and Control of NYC to end the euthanization of healthy and treatable cats and dogs in city animal shelters. The alliance works with organizations to increase pet adoptions and spay/neuter rates across the city, with the goal of ending all pet euthanasia in NYC by 2015.

Stephanie Mattera, spokeswoman for the Alliance, was introduced to Alex and Ani jewelry by friends who gave her a cat charm bangle for Christmas. She loved the piece, and after reading about the company online, was inspired to approach Carolyn about a partnership with Charity by Design. She sought out Nicki Castonguay, Vice President of Charity by Design, at an event and told her all about the Mayor's Alliance. Stephanie recalls, "When we started talking, there was instant synergy. Nicki was so passionate about animals, the environment, and giving back."

This conversation ended in a partnership that produced the Paw Print bangle, a charm that incorporates the Alliance's logo of a paw print in the shape of the New York skyline. In late fall to 2011, the bangle launched in Alex and Ani's SoHo store at a lively party that featured positive energy punch, and adoptable dogs on-site.

The bangle was a runaway success; it sold out online and in stores in two weeks; the funds raised far exceeded Stephanie's expectations. She says: "I'm just in awe of it. It's one of the best projects I've ever worked on, and the people at Alex and Ani really put their passion into it. The bangle allowed us to reach a new, nationwide audience of people who want to use their personal style to make a tangible statement about supporting animal welfare."

A dog for adoption at the Alex and Ani/ Mayor's Alliance event in New York

AFTERWORD

When I started working on this book, it was one project in a pile of freelance jobs - a writing contract for a company I'd heard of, but really didn't know much about.

As the project got going and I began to collect stories for the book, I was really moved by consistent themes defining the lives of the people I interviewed. I was surprised at how hard people were on themselves, yet impressed by the ways they used Alex and Ani to remind themselves to not just survive, but to smile. I met a mom who, in spite of the amazing amount of hard work she had to juggle on a daily basis as she cared for her children, was incredibly attractive and impeccably organized - yet she still felt her photos were unflattering, and that her home was too humble. I saw a student who, while intelligent, beautifully spoken and incredibly interesting, struggled with feelings of measuring up against a certain standard, one that might or might not actually even exist. I met people who learned lessons about death, happiness and gratitude by the guidance and struggles of close friends. I met young women who, though seemingly completely grounded, were still searching for an anchor, compass or path that would make everything around them make sense.

In each of these people I saw parts of myself, and subsequently embarked on my own journey to a deeper understanding of my motivations and my life's path. It was as if the people I interviewed held a mirror to my face, and the reality of my own struggles reflected back at me. It was incredibly powerful and affirming to hear these stories, and to look within myself to find how they could make me grow as a person.

This, along with interviewing Carolyn, listening to her stream of consciousness about her process and her ideas, made for a truly transformational experience. To frame the people I met through the lens of Carolyn's perspective on free will, positive thinking, having faith in your instincts and being true to what you know is your calling, it honestly couldn't have been better. I will never think of the phrase "words are powerful" the same way again. As I now move through my daily interactions with people, I much more fully understand the power of my words and intentions than I ever had before.

As Carolyn often says: "Take the journey, the rewards are great." I was an accidental, and somewhat reluctant participant on this journey, but in the end, I am eternally grateful for it, and will be reaping the rewards for years to come.

I am also eternally grateful to Alex Barbosa, who worked tirelessly on the design and layout of this book, and Elena Barkalova, who closely managed the entire endeavor. Their hard work, and that of the whole Alex and Ani team, made this production possible. Thank you all!

-Cyd

GIOVANNI FEROCE

Alex and Ani CEO

Alex and Ani CEO Giovanni Feroce is responsible for leading the company and successfully implementing strategic goals and objectives. With over 20 years of experience in the optical retail and consumer products industries, he provides leadership and direction toward achieving the company's philosophy, mission, strategy and annual revenue and growth goals. Prior to joining Alex and Ani, Mr. Feroce began cultivating his diverse leadership skills through politics and the military. He began his political career as the nation's youngest state senator, and went on to serve on the Rhode Island Senate committees on Corporations and on Labor. He also served as Secretary of the Joint Committee for Veteran's Affairs, and as Commissioner of the Rhode Island State Lottery. His military experience includes serving as a United States Army field-grade officer and Operation Iraqi Freedom Combat Veteran. Mr. Feroce's education includes the Wharton School - The University of Pennsylvania (Advanced Management Program), The University of Rhode Island (BA, Political Science) and The United States John F. Kennedy Special Warfare Center and School (Civil Affairs Officer Advance Course).

CYD MCKENNA

Alex and Ani Corporate historian and lifestyle editor

Cyd McKenna is the Corporate Historian and Lifestyle Editor at Alex and Ani. In addition to chronicling the evolution of the company, she is the editor of Life (+) Culture, Carolyn Rafaelian's lifestyle website. A Rhode Island native and graduate of Providence's Hope High School, Cyd holds a BA from San Francisco State University, a Master's Degree from MIT, and an Ed.M. from the Harvard Graduate School of Education. Currently, Cyd lives in Washington, D.C. with her two sons. She loves her camera, her voice recorder, and spotting and documenting great taste and style wherever she goes.

Charm Library

OM

CREATION | ONENESS | TRUTH

Om is an intonation, a sound resonating throughout the body into the soul. It signifies God, higher power, and the oneness of all beings in life's cycle. The past, the present, and the future are all represented in this one sound. Adorn yourself with the Om to connect with your inner spirit, accept serenity, and embrace your faith.

TURN PEACE UP®

KINDNESS | TRANQUILITY LIBERATION

A reminder to positively contribute to the world, Turn Peace Up® symbolizes the small actions that can be taken towards bettering humanity. Wear this charm to stand up for kindness and liberate the world from negativity.

STAR OF VENUS

LOVE | BEAUTY | INSPIRATION

Venus, the jewel of the sky, was once known as the morning and evening star because it shined the brighteSaint Associated also with the goddess of love, the Star of Venus Charm is a reminder to uncover your soul's beauty by allowing it to evolve and illuminate.

FOUR LEAF CLOVER

BLESSING | FORTUNE PROSPERITY

Carried by Eve from the Garden of Eden, the four leaf clover is traditionally associated with four blessings: faith, hope, love, and luck. Surrounded by the four alchemy symbols for the seasons, adorn yourself with the Four Leaf Clover Bangle charm to experience yearlong prosperity and fortune.

PATH OF LIFE

STRENGTH | MOTIVATION KNOWLEDGE

Emblematic of life's zenith and nadir moments, the Path of Life is representative of an infinite number of possibilities and expressions of love. Illustrating life's twists and turns, and unexpected winds, wear the Path of Life Charm to proudly celebrate your own willingness to travel towards life's fruitful moments.

TREE OF LIFE

HOPE | CONSERVATION GROWTH

The Tree of Life represents strong roots, consistent growth, and fruition. An acknowledgment of our commitment to nurture, love, and preserve the beauty of nature, wearing this charm evokes the eternal connection between mankind and Mother Earth.

ARMENIAN CROSS

LIFE | SPIRITUALITY IMMORTALITY

The ultimate cultural symbol, the cross symbolizes health, life, immortality, and the union of Heaven and Earth. Combining vines and floral trim with the traditional Christian cross, the unique Armenian Cross dates back to the 4th century. Wear this charm to honor your personal beliefs in the cross.

OPEN LOVE

ADMIRATION | JOY | LIGHT

Love is a virtue, an eternal gift given to others. Love is an admirable force that ignites our emotional center with passion, generosity, and affection. Love illuminates the spirit. Embrace the powers of your heart and share love openly for it is our core connections that cultivate happiness.

LOTUS PEACE PETALS

ILLUMINATION | BEAUTY RESILIENCE

With roots secured in the mud, a stem that grows through water, and a flower that lies pristinely above, the lotus signifies the progression of the soul. Inspiring us to rise from the darkness into enlightenment, the Lotus Peace Petals Charm also incorporates the higher power of a harmonious spirit with the Om symbol. Let this charm represent cognitive balance and spiritual growth.

EYE OF HORUS

PROTECTION | LIGHT | REASON

The left eye of the Egyptian God Horus is associated with lunar energy that symbolizes intuition, good health, and protection in connection with the moon. With the intention of safeguarding the king in the afterlife, the Eye of Horus is meant to ward off evil. Wear the Eye of Horus charm for healing properties, reasoning abilities, and powers of protection.

STAR OF DAVID

CREATION | SPIRITUALITY UNION

The symbol of Judaism, this six pointed star symbolizes the divine and perfect union of the masculine and feminine. The upward points recall masculine energy, the sun and fire; the downward points symbolize feminine energy, the moon and water. Wear this sacred symbol to evoke harmony and to celebrate faith.

CLADDAGH

LOVE | FRIENDSHIP | LOYALTY

The unique characteristics of the Claddagh design are associated with the virtues of love (the heart), loyalty (the crown), and friendship (the hands). Originating in the ancient village of Claddagh near Galway, Ireland, this symbol represents the intentions of the heart. Wear the Claddagh Charm to draw in your heart's desires.

FLEUR DE LIS

REGALITY | FAITH | RENEWAL

Traditionally used to represent French royalty, the Fleur de Lis symbolizes perfection, enlightenment, and life. The three petals are also associated with the protection of the Holy Tinity. Wear the Fleur de Lis as a representation of your faith in the changes and regeneration of life.

MOTHER MARY

GRACE | COMPASSION | HOPE

Blessed among women, Mother Mary represents extraordinary faith and the divine grace necessary to sacrifice everything. The epitome of love and mercy, she reminds us that the benefits of faith are infinite. Turn to Mother Mary as a source of hope and comfort in troubling times.

SAINT CHRISTOPHER

STRENGTH | PROTECTION | AID

Saint Christopher helped a child cross a river by bearing him on his back. Extraordinarily heavy, the child finally revealed himself as Jesus Christ who was carrying the weight of the world. Saint Christopher became the patron saint of travelers and a sacred source of protection.

SAINT ANTHONY

SELFLESSNESS | GUIDANCE ILLUMINATION

Saint Anthony of Padua, the patron saint of lost articles, guides us in locating and restoring all that is missing. Typically portrayed carrying the child Jesus, Saint Anthony encourages us to embrace the love of God. Carry Saint Anthony with you for divine direction and soulful enlightenment.

SEVEN SWORDS

LOVE | RADIANCE | STRENGTH

The seven swords represent the seven archangels: Michael, Jophiel, Chamuel, Gabriel, Raphael, Uriel and Zadkiel. Theirs is a world of love, symbolized by a radiant flame. Wear this charm to experience their higher power of love for yourself.

WELCOMING PINEAPPLE

WELCOME | WARMTH FRIENDSHIP

Expressing a sense of welcome, good cheer, and family affection, the pineapple signifies hospitality. New England sea captains traditionally placed a pineapple outside of their homes as a symbol of a safe return. Wear the Pineapple Charm to embrace friendships, celebrate homecomings, and encourage good times.

FEATHER

TRUTH | LIGHT | VIRTUE

An object representing light and air, a feather is the bearer of truth and justice. Ancient Egyptians believed a pure heart weighed as light as a feather. In Christianity, feathers represent virtues of charity, hope, and faith. Bestow the feather to seek wisdom and reach new heights.

WORLD PEACE

HARMONY | BALANCE TRANQUILITY

Positive energy is the key ingredient to creating world peace. Originally created as the symbol of a call for nuclear disarmament, the peace sign became synonymous with harmony, tranquility, and balance. Wearing this symbol spreads the harmonious message of peace.

CUPID'S HEART

LOVE | JOY | LIGHT

The heart is emblematic of so many things: love, sorrow, joy, affection, and compassion. It is symbolic of eternal bonds, desire, and spiritual aspirations. It is life. It is love. It is our emotional center. Wear Cupid's heart to find love or celebrate love.

OYSTER

TRUTH | REBIRTH | PURITY

To find an oyster beholding a pearl is a rare and blessed gift. Symbolizing true humility, the oyster proves that treasure lies within. Bestow the oyster and pearl to promote femininity, love, and inner beauty.

FRENCH ROYALTY

REGALITY | FAITH | RENEWAL

Traditionally used to represent French royalty, the Fleur de Lis is a symbol of perfection, enlightenment, and life. The three petals are also associated with the protection of the Holy Trinity. Wear the French Royalty Charm as a representation of your faith in the changes and regeneration of life.

NAUTICAL ANCHOR

HOPE | TRANQUILITY STABILITY

Holding fast and steady despite the elements, the anchor is a symbol of stability, hope, and peace. The anchor allows us to keep a clear mind amidst the tides of life. An emblem of good luck, wear the Nautical Anchor for courage, safety, and peace of mind.

STARFISH

VIGILANCE | INTUITION
ABILITY

The starfish is a resilient creature that constantly regenerates, intuitively navigates the sea, and directly impacts its ecological community. An ancient name for the Virgin Mary, the Star of the Sea symbolizes guidance, intuition, and vigilance. Wear the Starfish Charm for divine guided direction and a heightened sense of potential.

QUEEN'S CROWN

DIVINE RIGHT | QUEENSHIP
POWER

Known also as Great Mother, the queen represents feminine power and authority. She rules with values that inspire a kingdom or an individual to greatness. Wear this charm to help you assert your power, take charge of situations, and act with benevolence.

SKELETON KEY

POWER | CHOICE | LIBERATION

Keys unlock doors, revealing secrets and treasures within. A symbol of authority, keys represent the freedom to come and go without hindrance. Wear the key to unlock the secret places in your being. There you will find your most valuable treasures.

SAILBOAT

COURAGE | ADVENTURE
TRANSITION

A sailboat bestows peace to its wearer in times of change. Representing courage through transitional times, sailboats also symbolize the breath of the Holy Spirit. Wear the Sailboat Charm to celebrate the adventurous spirit that keeps you moving.

LUCKY CLOVER

LUCK | FORTUNE | PROSPERITY

The ultimate omen of good luck, finding a four leaf clover will bring good fortune to its finder. According to tradition, each leaf represents the virtues of faith, love, hope, and luck. Wear the Lucky Clover for increased luck and prosperity.

KEY TO MY HEART

SECRET | LOVE | SOUL

Locks protect one's secrets and desires. Only the key can unlock these spiritual aspirations unveiling our emotion center. Wear this charm with the intention of finding the spiritual key within.

SACRED DOVE

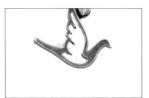

TRUTH | PEACE | FAITH

The classic symbol of the Holy Spirit, the dove is also synonymous with peace, faith, grace, and truth. On the occasion of John the Baptist's baptism of Jesus, it is written that the Holy Spirit, in the form of a dove, came down upon Jesus and remained with him. Wear this charm to express faith and hope.

KING'S CROWN

DIVINE RIGHT | KINGSHIP
POWER

A distinction of achievement, the crown is worn to express divine authority and honor. The king is a beacon of order, strength, and wisdom. Bestow the king's crown for increased power and integrity.

FISH

FERTILITY | CREATIVITY
TRANSFORMATION

The fish is a powerful and spiritual symbol in many religions. The ultimate symbol of rebirth and fertility, fish are also known to represent transformation. Wear the Fish Charm for adaptability, creativity, and the wisdom to successfully flow through life.

SEAHORSE

PATIENCE | PROTECTION
CONTENTMENT

In the belief that seahorses were a type of sea dragon, some Chinese cultures have revered them as a symbol of power and good luck. Their body structures only allow them to move in a very slow motion which has not evolved over time. They come to teach us patience and to accept ourselves as we are.

ENDLESS KNOT

WISDOM | COMPASSION
DESTINY

Representing the interweaving and ever-changing spiritual path, the Endless Knot expresses boundless wisdom and compassion. It illustrates an eternal pattern in its design, connecting one's destiny bound by time and change. Wear the Endless Knot Charm to remind you of life's journey and the entanglements of fate.

COMPASS

OBJECTIVE | DIRECTION
TRANSITION

An instrumental aid, a compass provides guidance and navigation through life's unexpected twists and turns. Each cardinal direction has a significant meaning. North represents home and infinite possibility. South embodies passion and the present. East signifies new beginnings and the future. West symbolizes emotion and the paSaint Wear the Compass Charm to guide you in the right direction.

DOLPHIN

COMMUNICATION | GRACE STRENGTH

Keeper of the sacred breath of life, the dolphin teaches us how to release emotions through our breath. The dolphin will also guide us into dreamtime so that we may access our own inner wisdom. It is whimsical and connects man to the world of the sea. This charm reminds us to breathe deeply and make time for play.

LOBSTER

CYCLES | REGENERATION PROTECTION

The lobster is associated with the cycles of the moon and ebb and flow of the tide. Lobsters cast off their shells for new ones. Guided by intuition, they know how to camouflage themselves when in danger. Wear the lobster and learn how to let go of the past, go with the flow, and protect yourself through life's changes.

MERMAID

FEMININITY | LOVE | MYSTERY

The mermaid is a combination of elemental and angelic energies. She is also known as a mistress of enchantment. Seductive and charming, all those in contact with the mermaid are subject to her persuasion. Wear this charm as you learn to unleash you own unique charm.

CONCH SHELL

POWER | AUTHORITY SOVEREIGNTY

The conch shell has served as the original trumpet since the beginning of time. Indian lore tells us that heroes of mythical warfare carried a mighty white conch shell. Its blast is believed to banish negative energy, avert natural disasters, and protect us from harm. Wear this charm for protection.

BUDDHA

HUMILITY | DEVOTION MEDITATION

Known as the Enlightened One, Buddha reminds us to be silent and go within. In doing so we have access to limitless power, limitless good karma, and limitless wisdom. He teaches us that the real secret to joy and happiness is to keep it simple.

SEASHELL

BEAUTY | INTUITION | LUCK

Seashells connect us to the ocean and to the water's energy. They enable us to gain clarity so that we make better decisions and life choices. They support, guide, and nudge us along our path to happiness and fulfillment. They bring about positive energy and promise fortunate outcomes in all areas of life.

APPLE BLOSSOM

ABUNDANCE | GODDESS | LOVE

Honored by Celts as a symbol of everlasting love, the apple blossom represents peace and affection. Intoxicating by nature, the Apple Blossom Charm reminds us to embrace our true passions to bring forth our inner goddess, achieve the impossible, and live with a loving, open heart.

DRAGONFLY

GRACE | CHANGE | POWER

Characterized by quick, sudden movements and a powerful wing stroke, the dragonfly uniquely changes direction on a whim. Symbolizing transition, the dragonfly has impeccable vision, which is a reminder to open one's eyes to the beauty of life's journey. Embrace the graceful energy of the dragonfly to live life to the fullest and to appreciate Mother Earth's gifts.

GRAPES

WISDOM | HOSPITALITY FORTUNE

A symbol of fertility, grapes are associated with good luck, hospitality, and pleasure. A historical icon, grapes represent the wine of life and immortality. Wear grapes to relax and enjoy life's fruitful moments.

APPLE OF ABUNDANCE

INSIGHT | WISDOM | TEACHER

A fruit that signifies intelligence, the apple is often associated with the ability to pass on knowledge to others. A teacher enlightens the soul and instills valuable information. Embrace the energy of the Apple of Abundance Charm for the guidance to accept the responsibility of sharing wisdom and passing it down from generation to generation.

WATER LILY

ENLIGHTENMENT | PURITY REBIRTH

Living in difficult conditions, the water lily is a symbol of beauty through turmoil. Rising above the water to extract energy from the sun, the water lily is a reminder that perseverance will lead to enlightenment and a reawakening. Embrace a sunny disposition and the purity of heart associated with the Water Lily Charm.

HUMMINGBIRD

AWAKENING | HEALING ETERNITY

With wings that flutter in the pattern of an infinity symbol, hummingbirds are associated with continuity, healing, and persistence. Delicate yet strong, the hummingbird actively seeks out the sweetest nectar representing our desire for the joyous gifts in life. Wear the Hummingbird Charm to be tenacious in the pursuit of dreams while keeping an open mind to spiritual awakenings.

BUMBLEBEE

*LOYAL | CONSCIENTIOUS
DRIVEN*

The bumblebee is hardworking and extraordinarily loyal to the Queen Bee and the entire community. A symbol of nature's perfect balance, the bee reminds us to slow down, smell the flowers, and taste the sweet honey of life. Wear the Bumblebee Charm to channel the bees' meticulous energy.

LADYBUG

LUCK | HAPPINESS | AFFECTION

Legend has it that the ladybug was named for the Virgin Mary who assisted farmers once they prayed to her. Keeping fields safe from harm, the ladybug evokes the energy of harmony. It teaches us to release worries and to enjoy experiences to the fulleSaint A messenger of promise, when the ladybug appears in our lives it is telling us to "let go and let God."

COUSIN

*SUPPORT | CONNECTION
EMPOWERMENT*

Inspiring and understanding, a cousin combines deep family bonds with authentic friendship. A flower of good cheer and happiness, the coreopsis empowers the wearer with optimism and a harmoniously clear state of mind. Embrace the heartfelt energy of an encouraging family dynamic.

MY OTHER HALF

*HARMONY | LOVE
COMPLETION*

To meet the fated completion of your soul is to find your other half. The camellia indicates the deep longing of the heart and its essence balances relationships. A harmonizing, devoted symbol, the My Other Half Charm celebrates the heart's undying strength and the infinite bond between two destined people.

SISTER

*IRREPLACEABLE | FOREVER
FRIEND*

Sisters possess an eternal connection, a forever friendship that can take on the world. Strong in good times and in bad, the honeysuckle consistently creates a sweet disposition to all those surrounded with it. A symbol of strength, adorn yourself with the Sister Charm to show appreciation and love for your irreplaceable sister.

AUNT

*ADMIRATION | CONNECTION
GRACE*

An eternal supporter and important role model, an aunt is a special person with whom you create everlasting memories. Symbolic of divine connection, the lavender exudes a strong yet graceful energy that transmits all that is negative into light. Give or wear the Aunt Charm as an illuminating symbol of admiration and to experience love's bright power.

NIECE

*OPTIMISTIC | BRIGHT
ENERGETIC*

Charmingly joyful, a niece is an energizing force of life. The sunflower, a powerhouse plant, encourages light to shine out from the soul. With an essence that warms peoples' hearts, give or wear the Niece Charm to celebrate the bright energy that flows from the flower of light.

DAUGHTER

*BLESSING | FRIEND
POSSIBILITY*

A daughter fills the world with beauty. She brings new life and embodies a dream of possibility for the future. The purity of a daisy is also associated with the discovery of love, much like a mother's sentiment towards her daughter. Give or wear the Daughter Charm for the girl who changes the world and makes every experience brighter.

MOM

GENEROSITY | HEROISM | LOVE

A mother's love and support is extraordinarily strong without limitation. The peony, the queen of the garden, symbolically encompasses the maternal traits of healing, love's blessing, and bravery. Embrace the heartfelt connection, strength, and respect associated with the Mom Charm as a token of admiration.

FRIEND

*LOYAL | INSPIRING
SUPPORTIVE*

A sincere confidante whose heart connects with your own, a friend is consistently loyal and encouraging. The ultimate emblem of friendship, the periwinkle, symbolizes eternity and the power of camaraderie. Give or wear the Friend Charm to honor the person that makes your soul blossom.

GODMOTHER

*INSPIRING | SPECIAL
PROTECTIVE*

A divinely chosen guardian, a Godmother is always there to consistently provide love and encouragement. Symbolic of affection and watchfulness, the violet emphasizes the loyal traits of a Godmother. Give or wear the Godmother Charm as a reminder that God chose this special person particularly for you.

GRANDMOTHER

WISE | GENEROUS | PROUD

A grandmother's eternal love carries on from generation to generation. Associated with divine holyones, the lily is a virtuous flower that stands for dignity and peace. Majestically beautiful, give or wear the Grandmother Charm to pay tribute to the honored matriarch whose pride and calming kindness is infinite.

JESUS

INSPIRATION | SPIRIT CONFIDENCE

Words when spoken hold powerful energy. Words when worn carry the same positive vibration. Alex and Ani's Words are Powerful Collection is intended to encourage inner strength and empower the wearer with positive energy.

LIVE A HAPPY LIFE

COURAGE | APPRECIATION CHOICE

Choose kindness, love and joy. Live life to the absolute fullest and open your mind up to spontaneous ideas. Live fearlessly, be optimistic, and become blissfully aware of life's gifts. Adorn yourself with the Live a Happy Life Charm to acknowledge the blessings in your existence and to be an inspiration to all.

EVERYTHING HAPPENS FOR A REASON

TRUST | FAITH | CONFIDENCE

As individuals that are significant parts of a greater plan, we must realize that everything happens for a reason. Eventually, everyone transforms into the unique person that they were destined to be. Adorn yourself with the Everything Happens for a Reason Charm, trust in fate, and allow life to take its course.

SWEET JESUS

HOPE | CONFIDENCE | FAITH

Sweet Jesus represents the courage it takes to believe in something higher than one's self. Sweet Jesus is a symbol of hope that all troubles will eventually be resolved proving that the benefits of faith are endless. Sweet Jesus provides the wearer with a sense of confidence and trust in spiritual conviction.

FASCINATE ME WITH LOVE

ENTHRALLING | EXCEPTIONAL INSPIRING

A limitless love is an enchanting and rare blessing. The thrill of an enduring love is exceptionally consuming and exhilarating. Wear this captivating charm as a proclamation to the world to "Fascinate Me with Love!"

THANK YOU

GRATITUDE | INFLUENCE HONOR

I appreciate you. You have positively influenced my life. The words of the heart express gratitude in many ways. Give or wear the Thank You Charm in honor of someone who has touched your heart.

IT IS WHAT IT IS

SPONTANEITY | BLESSING DESTINY

Sometimes life hands you the unexpected. Embrace these twists and turns as a divine blueprint that will lead you to your destined path and remember to appreciate the journey. Life is unpredictable. Life is an adventure. Life is a blessing. It is what it is and what you make it to be.

WHAT'S FOR YOU WILL NOT PASS YOU

OPTIMISM | DETERMINATION LIFE

Your life is destined for greatness. Obstacles will inevitably come your way. Greet them with patience and hard work. Allow the light of fated opportunities to spill through, live in fearlessness, and remember that what's for you will not pass you.

COMPLETELY BLESSED

FAITH | GRATITUDE | DIVINITY

All gifts in life come directly from above. Living in the present is the ultimate gift, full of promise and possibility. Allow yourself to be open to life's greatest moments without taking anything for granted. Seize your opportunities and realize that you are divinely and completely blessed everyday in every moment.

LAUGH

INSPIRATION | SPIRIT CONFIDENCE

Words when spoken hold powerful energy. Words when worn carry the same positive vibration. Alex and Ani's Words are Powerful Collection is intended to encourage inner strength and empower the wearer with positive energy.

IF IT'S MEANT TO BE

BELIEVE | TRUST | EMBRACE

Trust that you are exactly where you are supposed to be. Know in your heart that everything works itself out therefore there is no reason to worry. Enjoy the fact that you have been selected to be where you are in this moment. Embrace the energy of this charm as a reminder that we are all pieces of an interconnected plan and understand that your own perspective has a great effect on the outcome.

LIVE IN THE MOMENT

ENTHUSIASTIC | BOLD | ALIVE

Take today and make it count. Listen to your heart and take action now. Today is here. Tomorrow is not promised but is anticipated with much hope. All that you do, say, and feel sets the stage for the future so remember that this moment has the power to ensure tomorrow's happiness. Adorn yourself with the Live in the Moment Charm to open yourself up to the opportunities in today.

| SPIRITUAL ARMOR |

ARMENIAN CROSS WRAP

*LIFE | SPIRITUALITY
IMMORTALITY*

The ultimate cultural symbol, the cross, symbolizes health, life, immortality, and the union of heaven and Earth. Combining vines and floral trim with the traditional Christian cross, the unique Armenian Cross dates back to the 4th century. Wear this to honor your personal beliefs in the cross.

QUILL FEATHER WRAP

TRUTH | FAITH | VIRTUE

An object representing light and air, a feather is the bearer of truth and justice. Ancient Egyptians believed a pure heart weighed as light as a feather. In Christianity, feathers represent virtues of charity, hope, and faith. Bestow the feather to seek wisdom and reach new heights.

BAMBOO WRAP

LUCK | OPTIMISM | LONGEVITY

Referred to as a tree of good omens, bamboo symbolizes longevity, luck, and a sacred barrier against evil. Wear the Spirtual Armor Bamboo Wrap to enhance your resilience and surround yourself with positive omens.

PHOENIX WRAP

*REBIRTH | SACRIFICE
IMMORTALITY*

The Phoenix, a mythical sacred firebird, is known to rise from its ashes in regeneration. An emblem of divinity, loyalty, and immortality, the Spiritual Armor Phoenix Wrap reminds us that change is good for the soul.

LIGHTNING WRAP

AWAKENING | CHANGE | FATE

A symbol of power and sudden breakthrough, lightning represents a swift awakening. Adorn yourself with the Lightning Wrap to initiate change, mark destiny, and address chance happenings.

PLUME FEATHER WRAP

TRUTH | FAITH | VIRTUE

An object representing light and air, a feather is the bearer of truth and justice. Ancient Egyptians believed a pure heart weighed as light as a feather. In Christianity, feathers represent virtues of charity, hope, and faith. Bestow the feather to seek wisdom and reach new heights.

OM WRAP

CREATION | ONENESS | TRUTH

Om is an intonation, a sound resonating throughout the body into the soul. It signifies God, higher power, and the oneness of all beings in life's cycle. The past, the present, and the future are all represented in this one sound. Adorn yourself with the Om to connect with your inner spirit, accept serenity, and embrace your faith.

TRIDENT WRAP

*INFLUENCE | PROGRESSION
PROTECTION*

A symbol of authority, the trident was historically connected to Poseidon, the Greek god of water, the sea, and storms. Channel your individual power to contribute positively in all aspects of life. Wear the Trident Wrap for understanding, protection, and positive energy.

GREEK KEY WRAP

*FRIENDSHIP | ETERNITY
STRENGTH*

The Greek Key, also known as the Meander, was the most important symbol in Ancient Greece, symbolizing infinity and eternal bonding. Often given as a gift, the Spiritual Armor Greek Key represents bonds of friendship, love, and unending devotion.

CROSS WRAP

LIFE | UNION | IMMORTALITY

The Cross Wrap represents the union of the concepts of divinity. The cross is one of the most ancient human symbols, and is used by many religions to represent the crucifixion of Jesus ChriSaint Symbolizing health, fertility, life, immortality, the union of heaven and earth, and the spirit and matter, wear this bangle to honor your personal beliefs in the cross.

PEACOCK FEATHER WRAP

TRUTH | FAITH | VIRTUE

An object representing light and air, a feather is the bearer of truth and justice. Ancient Egyptians believed a pure heart weighed as light as a feather. In Christianity, feathers represent virtues of charity, hope, and faith. Bestow the feather to seek wisdom and reach new heights.

ATLANTEAN WRAP

*PROTECTION | KNOWLEDGE
HEALING*

The power of an Atlantis symbol lies in the symbol itself that disperses negative energy and provides well being by connecting the wearer to higher vibrations. Archaeologist Howard Carter wore the Atlantean symbol while excavating King Tut's tomb. Many believe this symbol protected him from a mythic pharaoh's curse, which caused the other excavators' untimely deaths. Wear the Atlantean Symbol for healing energy, to protect yourself from negative influences, and to embrace psychic knowledge.

ENDLESS KNOT WRAP

WISDOM | COMPASSION
DESTINY

Symbolizing boundless wisdom, the Endless Knot reminds us of the entanglements of fate. Adorn yourself with the Spiritual Armor Endless Knot to navigate the twists of life's journey and to maintain understanding of the interwoven beauty and strength of the human spirit.

WATER WRAP

PEACEFUL | IMAGINATIVE
EMOTIONAL

Water is a mediator, known primarily for its serene nature and open mind. Passionate and creative, Water is ever changing and unafraid of self-expression.

AIR WRAP

ADAPTABLE | INTELLIGENT
SPIRITUAL

Quick and animated, Air is known for originality, acceptance, and versatility. Air appreciates different perspectives, believes in the protection of higher powers, and values expressions of love.

EARTH WRAP

GROUNDED | LOYAL | RATIONAL

Thoughtful and reliable, Earth cares deeply for others without judgment. Earth is patient, compassionate, and sees all aspects of life through to completion.

FIRE WRAP

INDIVIDUALITY | PASSION
ENERGY

Spontaneous Fire applies its energies wholeheartedly in all aspects of life. Imaginative and innovative, Fire uses its zeal to pursue creativity.

SWORD OF ARCHANGEL
MICHAEL WRAP

ILLUMINATION | PROTECTION
FAITH

Victorious in all spiritual battles, Saint Michael is usually depicted with unsheathed sword in hand. Symbolizing enlightenment and powerful protection, the Sword of Archangel Michael guarantees the wearer success in all endeavors with the knowledge that a higher power always triumphs.

SNAKE COIL WRAP

RENEWAL | HEALING
PROTECTION

The snake is a symbol of regeneration, rebirth, and healing powers. Wear the Snake Coil to embrace change and the rejuvenation of life.

ANKH WRAP

ETERNITY | CONTINUITY
SALVATION

The Ankh Wrap is an ancient, Egyptian cross symbolizing eternal life. It celebrates the Divine Feminine, the Holy Masculine and communion. Unity of feminine and masculine is implicit in its form: the feminine loop and the masculine staff together render it the Key of Life.

| PLACES WE LOVE |

NANTUCKET ISLAND

*CONSERVATION | CULTURE
TRANQUILITY*

The sparkling waters of the Nantucket Sound mixed with the historical integrity and tranquil atmosphere attract thousands of visitors each year. With over 40 percent of the island sanctioned as protected conservation land, the eco-conscious inhabitants of Nantucket appreciate the rare habitats and species found in this visually stunning region.

NYC SUBWAY TOKEN

*TRADITION | CONNECTION
JOURNEY*

This New York City subway token design will bring you back to classic New York circa 1950. One of the oldest and busiest subways in the world, the New York Subway connects millions of people everyday. Reminisce on past experiences and celebrate your future by wearing the NYC Subway Token.

SAN FRANCISCO

DIVERSITY | LOVE | FREEDOM

San Francisco is home to the social phenomena known as the Summer of Love. Today the refreshing summer air, steep rolling hills, and famous landmarks create a diverse and loving feeling within this city. The iconic Golden Gate Bridge is the focal point of the San Francisco charm, a reminder that significant connections are at the core of our spirits.

MARTHA'S VINEYARD

PRISTINE | UNIQUE | PEACEFUL

This tiny, vibrant island off of Cape Cod boasts unparalleled, pristine beaches and picturesque views. Martha's Vineyard is the ultimate summer spot to relax, reenergize, and embrace nature's beauty. Wear this charm to show your love for Martha's Vineyard.

BLOCK ISLAND

*CAREFREE | TRANQUIL
NATURAL*

An island rich in pristine beaches and spectacular bluffs, Block Island is a hidden gem in the Atlantic. The island serves as an invitation to embrace a blissful outlook and to simply relax in the unparalleled beauty that Mother Nature has created. With preserved open spaces, Block Island emphasizes the importance of conservancy as a reminder that the world is what we make of it.

EDGARTOWN LIGHTHOUSE

*TRADITIONAL | CHARMING
ILLUMINATING*

The first colony on Martha's Vineyard, Edgartown is known primarily for its preserved 19th century seaport, picturesque harbor, and whaling traditions. Depicted on an Expandable Wire Bangle, the Edgartown Lighthouse is a beacon of light for generations of sailors and a popular point of interest for all seasonal guests. Wear this charm to show your love for Edgartown and its historic lighthouse.

BOSTON

PROUD | DISTINCT | HISTORIC

Boston is one of the oldest cities in the United States, combining the historic quality of early America with the modern landscape of today. The largest city in New England, Boston boasts a bustling, urban community that is unequivocally spirited and proud. Embrace the feisty, loyal energy of the Boston Charm to showcase the beauty of its distinct city scape.

WASHINGTON, D.C.

FREEDOM | PRIDE | HERITAGE

Our nation's beloved capital, Washington, D.C., represents our extraordinary patriotism as a united country. A plethora of significant landmarks showcase our country's democratic heritage. The Washington Monument, the White House, and the U.S. Capitol Building are all depicted on the Washington, D.C. Charm as a reminder of the heroic events that changed the course of our history.

LOS ANGELES

*IMAGINATION | GLITZ
ICONOGRAPHY*

The Creative Capital of the World, Los Angeles is home to one of the most iconic attractions, the Hollywood Walk of Fame. This landmark showcases an abundance of talented artists in the motion picture, music, and television industries. The legendary Hollywood Boulevard encourages you to nurture your imagination and chase your dreams.

MIAMI

OPTIMISTIC | ARTISTIC | VIBRANT

Home to South Beach, Miami is known for its tropical weather, art deco buildings, and exciting nightlife. Its unique culture and upbeat atmosphere create a one-of-a kind city that reflects the vibrant diversity of America. Channel the sunny, enthusiastic energy of the Miami Charm to stay positive and view all experiences as opportunities.

NEWPORT

TRANQUIL | HISTORIC | SCENIC

Newport is the home of Alex and Ani. With amazing beaches, beautiful mansions, and historic colonial landscapes, Newport creates a picturesque ambiance unlike any other. The Newport Bridge, an impressive and essential element of the skyline, is depicted on this charm as a reminder of the city's peaceful setting and its diverse array of possibilities.

NEW YORK SKYLINE

*RESILIENCE | ENERGY
OPTIMISM*

The Big Apple's skyline is universally recognized with the most notable skyscraper in the world, the Empire State Building, standing strong. Embrace the bold energy of the New York Skyline Charm to follow your wildest dreams and to reach for the biggest opportunities in the world.

SAINT ANTHONY

*SELFLESSNESS | GUIDANCE
ILLUMINATION*

Saint Anthony of Padua, the patron saint of lost articles, guides us in locating and restoring all that is missing. Typically portrayed carrying the child Jesus, Saint Anthony encourages us to embrace the love of God and find the words of God in our hearts. Carry Saint Anthony with you for divine direction and soulful enlightenment.

SAINT CHRISTOPHER

STRENGTH | PROTECTION | AID

Saint Christopher helped a child cross a river by bearing him on his back. Extraordinarily heavy, the child finally revealed himself as Jesus Christ who was carrying the weight of the world. Saint Christopher became the patron saint of travelers and a sacred source of protection.

SAINT MICHAEL

CHIVALRY | PROTECTION | VALOR

Archangel Michael's name means "Who is like God." He was the field commander of God's army and has come to be known as the patron saint of authority figures and militia. Wear this protective charm to rise above the negative forces in your life for it was Michael's likeness to God and great love that vanquished evil.

SAINT FRANCIS OF ASSISI

*GENEROSITY | AWARENESS
BENEVOLENCE*

The patron saint of animals and the environment, Saint Francis of Assisi preached about the responsibility humans had to protect and nourish the environment and all of God's creatures. His mystical experiences and compassionate nature teach us to have faith in a higher power, share kindness with all beings, and contribute our energy to positively improve the world.

MOTHER MARY

GRACE | COMPASSION | HOPE

Blessed among women, Mother Mary represents extraordinary faith and the divine grace necessary to surrender everything. The epitome of love and mercy, she reminds us that the benefits of faith are infinite. Turn to Mother Mary as a source of hope and comfort in troubling times.

SAINT JUDE THADDEUS

HOPE | TRUST | ENLIGHTENMENT

One of the Twelve Apostles of Jesus, Saint Jude Thaddeus is the helper and keeper of the hopeless. The patron saint of desperate cases, he gives wisdom, offers hope, and creates confidence. Turn to Saint Jude Thaddeus to guide you through difficult situations for he provides the optimism necessary to succeed.

SAINT FLORIAN

TRUTH | BRAVERY | FAITH

A courageous symbol for the faithful, Saint Florian is said to have saved a burning village with a bucket of water. He proves that bravery is the only necessity to face the impossible and succeed. The patron saint of firefighters, he encourages us to stand strong, rise up to defend our beliefs, and face life boldly. Channel the energy of Saint Florian for the power to speak and live the truth.

SAINT JOSEPH

GUIDANCE | FAITH | WISDOM

Husband of the Virgin Mary and the earthly father of Jesus, Saint Joseph is the patron saint of workers. A man of devoted faith, he turned to the angels for protecting and guiding his son. Look to Saint Joseph for the divine wisdom to lead you in the right direction.

| BIRTHSTONES |

GARNET

JANUARY

*CREATIVITY | PATIENCE
PERSEVERANCE*

A fiery royal stone, January's garnet is a sign of passion, good luck, and motivation. Wear the royal garnet to stimulate the senses and increase vitality.

AMETHYST

FEBRUARY

LOVE | HARMONY | SERENITY

A stone of wisdom, February's amethyst draws forth one's intuition in order to bring clarity to emotions, feelings, and values. Wear amethyst to ward off guilt and fear allowing calm to break through.

AQUAMARINE

MARCH

PEACE | COURAGE | HEALTH

The most powerful meditation stone, March's aquamarine brings great peace, serenity, and harmony. Wear aquamarine to clear the mind and build courage.

CRYSTAL

APRIL

SPIRIT | LOVE | STRENGTH

Known as a stone of affection, April's crystal is associated with independence, youth, and enthusiasm. Wear the crystal to exude passion in all endeavors and to maintain powerful inner strength.

EMERALD

MAY

LOVE | WISDOM | GROWTH

A sacred stone of the goddess Venus, May's emerald is thought to preserve love. A symbol of hope, wear the emerald to grow spiritually and to seek inner wisdom.

LIGHT AMETHYST

JUNE

*FAITH | PROTECTION
STRENGTH*

A protective amulet, June's light amethyst is used to guard against guilt and uncertainty. Signifying courage and empowerment, wear light amethyst as a guard against fear and uncertainty.

RUBY

JULY

*PASSION | CONTENTMENT
LOVE*

A symbol of vitality and royalty, July's ruby is the most powerful of all gems. Symbolizing deep love and passion, the ruby is known to bring peaceful contentment to the wearer.

PERIDOT

AUGUST

PEACE | LUCK | COURAGE

A power stone, August's peridot fosters emotional balance and the strength to create a bright future. Known also as the evening emerald for its light green color, peridot is a symbol of opportunity and prosperity.

SAPPHIRE

SEPTEMBER

*CLARITY | WISDOM
TRANQUILITY*

Known as the stone of destiny, September's sapphire is a symbol of optimism and serenity. Wear sapphire to clear your mind of clutter and to embrace fate.

ROSE

OCTOBER

*LOVE | HARMONY
COMPASSION*

Known as the love stone, October's rose allows the wearer to continually give affection and express adoration. Wear the rose birthstone to motivate kindness, forgiveness, and compassion.

TOPAZ

NOVEMBER

*COURAGE | FIDELITY
WISDOM*

Know as the stone of true love and success, November's topaz is said to encourage self-realization and confidence. Wear topaz for increased strength and intellect in matters of the heart.

BLUE ZIRCON

DECEMBER

*FORTUNE | HAPPINESS
INTUITION*

A stone of stability, December's blue zircon has been known to promote wisdom and uplift the mind. Wear blue zircon to promote spiritual growth, optimism, and prosperity.

| ZODIACS |

AQUARIUS

JANUARY 20 - FEBRUARY 18

HUMANITARIAN
INDIVIDUALISTIC | ECLECTIC

Aquarius is an independent, original thinker whose ideas may seem unconventional but clearly are the products of a steady, thoughtful mind. The water bearer is resolute, capable not only of conceiving the big ideas but also seeing them to fruition.

PISCES

FEBRUARY 19 - MARCH 20

IMAGINATIVE | COMPASSIONATE
INTUITIVE

Creative and highly intuitive, Pisces is the most artistic of all the signs and highly adept at understanding people. While they are exceedingly sensitive and compassionate, the fish are also elusive and emotional extremists.

ARIES

MARCH 21 - APRIL 19

ADVENTUROUS | DYNAMIC
COURAGEOUS

Fiery, passionate Aries has the courage to love and to be loved. Arians are driven and generally impulsive individuals. The ram is known for its enthusiasm, energy, and excitement for all of life's adventures.

TAURUS

APRIL 20 - MAY 20

PERSISTENT | DETERMINED
STRONG

The Taurus is known for steadfastness and strength. A loyal companion, the bull has a passion for all things beautiful. The Taurus is extremely persistent yet appreciative and loving.

GEMINI

MAY 21 - JUNE 20

VERSATILE | COMMUNICATIVE
INQUISITIVE

An unpredictable nature and a quick wit make the Gemini anything but dull. The charming twins possess an inquisitive personality that keeps them in a constant search to appease their ever-changing curiosities. The Gemini is also known to inspire others since their charisma and achievements are infectious.

CANCER

JUNE 21 - JULY 22

PROTECTIVE | SENSITIVE
CHANGEABLE

Traditionalist Cancers love their families. They are domestic nesters and homebodies who devote their energies to creating an environment that is warm, loving, and inviting. The crab is identified with the tranquil essence of water and is known for its fidelity and sensitivity.

LEO

JULY 23 - AUGUST 22

DOMINANT | EXTROVERTED
LOYAL

Reliable Leo is used to being the center of attention. Confidence emanates from the Leo and manifests itself in dramatic gestures. Their bold, outgoing natures are tempered with genuine kindness.

SCORPIO

OCTOBER 23 – NOVEMBER 21

PASSIONATE | EXCITING
POWERFUL

Scorpios are inquisitive. They seek to know life's mysteries and secrets. Intense and private, Scorpios prefer to share their thoughts with a select few. Those who are taken into their confidence are blessed for Scorpios are extremely loyal to friends.

LIBRA

SEPTEMBER 23 - OCTOBER 22

FAIR | BALANCED
HARMONIOUS

Libras are the antidote to conflict. Objective and just, Libras make wonderful moderators and judges. Always the diplomat, Libra is the champion of harmony and the nemesis of discord. The Libra's natural charm makes resolution not only possible but also pleasant.

VIRGO

AUGUST 23 - SEPTEMBER 22

REFINED | METICULOUS
DILIGENT

Private and pragmatic, Virgo believes in preparedness. Attention to detail is a strength of Virgos and their output reflects this virtue. They are hard workers who tend to err on the side of caution.

SAGITTARIUS

NOVEMBER 22 - DECEMBER 21

LOVING | PHILOSOPHICAL
RESTLESS

Wild child Sagittarius loves to explore, to learn and to grow. The archer meets the world with the spirit of an adventurer and the mind of a scholar. For Sagittarius, life is a grand adventure and possibilities await at every turn.

CAPRICORN

DECEMBER 22 - JANUARY 19

AMBITIOUS | PATIENT
HUMOROUS

Success is the Capricorn's birthright. Earthy and industrious, the resolute Capricorn can expect hard work to be rewarded. The goat is cautious, watchful and deliberate and acts in a manner reflective of a disciplined character.

TURTLE SPIRIT

MOTHER EARTH | GROUNDING
PATIENCE

Carrying its home with it for protection, the turtle embodies the gifts of the Earth and is a reminder to take care of the environment and appreciate all of its blessings. Patient, gentle, and determined, the turtle overcomes obstacles one step at a time. Embrace the Turtle Spirit for a connection to Earth's wisdom.

BEAR SPIRIT

INTROSPECTIVE | STRONG
REGENERATIVE

The spirit of the bear is a protective source of strength and healing. The strong bear is a cave dweller that knows when to retreat into the womb of Mother Earth for introspection and rest. Let the energy of the Bear Spirit be a source of spiritual, physical, and emotional regeneration.

HAWK SPIRIT

MESSENGER | PERSPECTIVE
INSPIRATION

Carrying messages from the Great Spirit to the people, a hawk is known for its keen senses and effortless flight. A feather bestows the wearer with insight that comes from expanded perspective that helps one soar to great heights. Embrace the vision, inspiration, and innovation carried forward from the Hawk Spirit.

WOLF SPIRIT

TEACHER | PATHFINDER
LOYAL

Known as the great teacher, the wolf is independent yet fiercely loyal to its pack. Boldly taking new directions and exploring unfamiliar territories, the wolf's curiosity leads to spiritual discovery. Seek out the Wolf Spirit for guidance in new endeavors and the bravery to move forward.

APPLE TREE

CREATIVITY | LOVE
ABUNDANCE

Abundantly strong, the apple tree is highly valued due to its ability to replenish and regenerate each season. Known as the mystical tree of Avalon, the apple tree has a long history connected to divine feminine principles and the capabilities of the imagination. A symbol of spiritual sustenance, channel the energy of the Apple Tree Charm to nourish your soul.

OAK TREE

STABILITY | POWER | ENERGY

A symbol of courage and a storehouse of wisdom, the oak is the mightiest of trees. Ancients believed that the oak's leaves had a multitude of powers that could heal and renew a tired spirit. Embrace the strong energy of the Oak Tree Charm for the power to stand strong with an enthusiastic disposition.

ASH TREE

CONNECTION | WISDOM
GROWTH

The ash is a healing tree of possibility. Its energy is one of growth, expansion, and higher perspective. It is a reminder that with great achievement and high attainment, we need to stay grounded and well rooted in our path. Utilize the power of the Ash Tree Charm to cultivate your individual journey to the height of your dreams.

FIR TREE

RESILIENCE | CLARITY
LONGEVITY

The fir is evergreen, keeping its energy flowing through all seasons. A symbol of endurance and hope, the fir tree is steadfast in all conditions as it survives the environment's temperaments. A forthright tree that grows straight and narrow, channel the energy of the Fir Tree Charm to stand tall in your endeavors and to greet each challenge with a resilient spirit.

WILLOW TREE

SOULFUL | FLEXIBLE
INTUITIVE

With sizable roots and a tenacious lifespan, the willow is naturally, intuitively strong. An adaptable tree that can bend without snapping, the willow is a reminder to stay true to your core while adjusting with life's turns. Embrace the energy of the Willow Tree Charm to keep growing and reaching higher no matter where you are planted.

CHARITY
— BY —
DESIGN

EMPOWERMENT | LOVE
COMMUNITY

Charity by Design empowers non-profit organizations to reach their goals by capturing the power of positive energy through innovative, creative designs. Proceeds are donated directly to each organization, enabling them to positively contribute to the lives of others and make our world a better place.

YOUNG & STRONG

Dana Farber Cancer Institute

FAITH | HOPE
DETERMINATION

The Young & Strong symbol is a tribute to remarkable women of courage. Wear this charm as inspiration to embrace peace, love, and healing through the power of positive thinking.

SHARK FINN

Finnz Funz

STABILITY | PROTECTION
COURAGE

The shark fearlessly navigates through all situations and confidently moves forward in life. With a distinctive fin located on its back for stability, a shark retains its balance and is equipped to handle any sudden twists and turns. Allow the energy of the Shark Finn Charm to guide you through life's ever changing waters.

| CHARITY BY DESIGN |

HOPE

Gloria Gemma Breast Cancer Resource Foundation

STRENGTH | FAITH | COURAGE

To believe in something beyond reason, to aspire for greatness beyond imagination, and to expect positive outcomes against the odds is to possess hope. Carry it with you in all of life's experiences and understand that hope is a blessing that leads to inner peace.

BUTTERFLY

Hanley and Caron Treatment Centers

RENEWAL | STRENGTH | REBIRTH

A regenerative species, butterflies consistently transition from caterpillar to cocoon to butterfly. Giving us faith in change, the butterfly is associated with unwavering grace, soulful insight, and eloquence on our journey. Channel the energy of the butterfly and emerge brilliantly from your own transformation.

TODAY IS AN OPPORTUNITY

Pancreatic Cancer Action Network

COURAGE | APPRECIATION INFLUENCE

Opportunity is here; invite it in. In this moment you can choose to take action and contribute your gifts of courage, kindness, and love. You have the ability to allow your light to shine and illuminate another. Today is an opportunity to lead, to inspire, to volunteer, to make a difference.

BORN TO BE SOMETHING

KIPP, NY

ASPIRE | LEARN | EMPOWER

Gifted and unique, you have the power to shine. Acknowledge your calling and become exactly who you were created to be. Collaborate, learn, and work hard, for you were born to be something extraordinary.

MY LOVE IS ALIVE

Tuesday's Children

RESILIENCE | SPIRIT EMPOWERMENT

Ignite your heart with love, the power to let your past change the future. You were born with the strength to shine your light in the darkest places. Embrace and reflect the love that others shine upon you, for love is our common bond.

PHOENIX

Home and Hospice Care of Rhode Island

DIVINITY | REBIRTH IMMORTALITY

The phoenix, a mythical and sacred fire bird, is known to rise from its ashes in regeneration. With strong wings to soar to great heights, it represents a new life filled with opportunity. An emblem of divinity and immortality, the Phoenix Charm reminds us that change is good for the soul.

THE ELEPHANT

Friends of Jaclyn

LUCK | INSPIRATION | LOYALTY

The elephant walks through life with family close by in a loyal and dedicated manner. Extraordinarily protective, elephants are known to stand up for others encouraging the values of camaraderie, perseverance, and unity. With a trunk up for luck, wear The Elephant Charm to inspire others to pursue their passions and embrace the power of teamwork.

PAW PRINT

Mayor's Alliance for NYC's Animals

COMPASSION | OPTIMISM APPRECIATION

Significant parts of our culture, pets are loyal companions that seek love. Optimistically the day will come when all dogs and cats have a loving home and family to belong to. Wear the Paw Print charm and help to make this dream a reality for thousands of animals.

TREE HUGGER

African Rainforest Conservancy

CONSCIOUS | PROTECTIVE |ENVIRONMENTALIST

With an awareness of the social, ecological, and environmental benefits of trees, a tree hugger appreciates nature's blessings. Equipped with the knowledge that the world is what you make of it, a tree hugger moves forward in life consciously, always aware of the importance of an environment. Embrace the organic energy of the Tree Hugger Charm as a reminder to protect our plant.

CUPCAKE

Nancy Davis Foundation

SWEET | DIVINE | OPTIMISTIC

A rush of sugar can provide bliss and harmony on the most challenging of days. Cupcakes symbolize the importance of celebrating life's little moments and the joys of all things decadent. Adorn yourself with the Cupcake Charm to embrace an optimistic outlook that leads to a peaceful existence.

18TH HOLE

Traveler's Championship

ENJOYMENT | DEDICATION PATIENCE

An unpredictable game focused on camaraderie and competition, golf puts an emphasis on enjoyment and self-improvement. Wear the 18th Hole Charm as a representation of your own personal journey and as a reminder that golf, like life, is what you make it.

LET CREATIVITY RULE

Unified Theater

ABILITY | ARTISTRY COLLABORATION

We have the capability to create, inspire, and bring dreams to fruition. We succeed when we let our intuition run wild. We embrace outlandish ideas to design relatable art. We encourage imagination. We empower the right sides of our brains. We let creativity rule.

HERO

Hasbro Children's Hospital

**INSPIRATION | COURAGE
ADMIRATION**

Heroes come in all shapes and sizes; they are the people who empower and impact the lives around them through their compassion and courage. Wearing this bangle represents the hero in you as a supporter of Hasbro Children's Hospital and their efforts to provide world class care to children.

LIVE MUSIC

Newport Festivals Foundation

**INSPIRATION | CREATIVITY
TRADITION**

The exhilaration of live music stays with us long after the final notes have been played. Inspiring creative freedom, the musical traditions of folk and jazz music continue to evolve today. Support today's creative artists in an effort to educate young people about folk and jazz traditions while keeping the music alive.

PIECE OF THE PUZZLE

National Autism Association

**INDIVIDUALITY | DISCOVERY
UNITY**

Like a puzzle piece, every individual is shaped differently with unique talents, perspectives and beliefs. Once we share these gifts with each other, positivity will spread and hope will endure. Embrace the energy of the Piece of the Puzzle Charm and realize that we are all interwoven parts of a greater masterpiece.

RIBBON OF STRENGTH

Gloria Gemma Breast Cancer Resource Foundation

**AWARENESS | HOPE
EMPOWERMENT**

A band of inspiration, the Ribbon of Strength is a recognizable sign of the fight against cancer and the power of a resilient spirit. Wear this ribbon to encourage awareness, inspire action, and empower others.

GIFT BOX

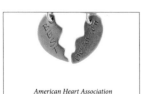

American Cancer Society

**CONNECTION | JOY
GRATITUDE**

Life is for filling days with celebrations, enjoying the smallest happiness, and cherishing every shared second with the people you love. Proudly acknowledge the achievements and milestones of each day with the understanding that every moment is a blessing. Wrap your life in festivity and appreciate the joys of a gift box, for today is the ultimate present.

BECAUSE I AM A GIRL

Plan International USA

**EMPOWERMENT | POSITIVITY
CHANGE**

Because I am a girl, I am born to nurture. I am born to love. I am instinctual and perfectly in tune with nature. I am born to achieve. I am capable. I am brace. I am born to inspire others and I am a blessing to the world.

LOTUS BLOSSOM

Women & Infants Hospital

**STRENGTH | ETERNITY
CONNECTION**

A celebration of the female spirit, the Lotus Blossom is a symbol of beauty, strength, and grace. The strong stem's connection to the flower represents an eternal, unbreakable bond between two people. Spiritually enlightening and divinely beautiful, the Lotus Blossom Charm reminds us that our relationships and shared hearts are the key to happiness.

IT'S NOT A SPRINT

Dana Farber Cancer Institute

**PERSISTENCE | STRENGTH
HEART**

In the beginning of a marathon, your head keeps you focused with the notion that all dreams are possible with the right state of mind. As the journey progresses, the sheer will to succeed must move you forward. At the most challenging moments, your heart will undoubtedly take over. Adorn yourself with this charm as a reminder that life is the ultimate marathon

BEST FRIENDS

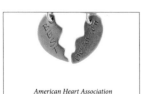

American Heart Association

**LOYALTY | HAPPINESS
INFINITY**

The heart is at the core of our spiritual and emotional center. To share your heart with another is to create an unbreakable bond of kindness, trust, and love. Share your affection and your charm with the Best Friends Bangle Set.

CORNUCOPIA

Blessings in a Backpack

**GENEROUS | BOUNTIFUL
BLESSING**

A symbol of abundance, the cornucopia signifies all of the sustainable blessings that Mother Nature provides. Mythically created with Zeus' goat's horn, the cornucopia is an inexhaustible horn of plenty that reminds us to appreciate all of life's gifts.

STAND UP

Stand Up to Cancer

**COLLABORATE | HONOR
CHANGE**

In this moment lives are transforming. People are uniting, standing up to better the world, and protecting the future. Together we are unstoppable. Join the movement and stand up to pioneer new pathways and accelerate positive change.

LIVING WATER

Living Water International

**PURITY | HEALING
REFLECTION**

Everything begins with water. It is the most precious resource that supports life in all of its forms. Water is the nourishment that mends us - body and soul. A purifying symbol, the Living Water Charm was created for daily reflection - leading us to the type of compassion and healing that quenches the thirst of the world.

MAJOR LEAGUE BASEBALL™

MOTIVATION | HEART PATRIOTISM

A symbol of American identity, baseball has long been known for it's outward expression of the drive that leads to victory. Adorn yourself with the Major League Baseball™ Charms for the motivation and inspiration to succeed in the game of life.

LOS ANGELES ANGELS™

LOS ANGELES DODGERS™

SAN DIEGO PADRES™

MIAMI MARLINS ™

MINNESOTA TWINS ™

SEATTLE MARINERS™

SAN FRANCISCO GIANTS™

NEW YORK YANKEES ™

PITTSBURGH PIRATES ™

KANSAS CITY ROYALS™

MILWAUKEE BREWERS™

OAKLAND ATHLETICS ™

NEW YORK METS ™

TEXAS RANGERS™

TORONTO BLUE JAYS™

PHILADELPHIA PHILLIES ™

NEW YORK YANKEES ™

TAMPA BAY RAYS™

SAINT LOUIS CARDINALS™

| CHARITY BY DESIGN |

ATLANTA BRAVES™

CHICAGO WHITE SOX™

BALTIMORE ORIOLES™

COLORADO ROCKIES™

CHICAGO CUBS™

CLEVELAND INDIANS™

ALL STAR GAME 2012

CINCINNATI REDS™

ARIZONA DIAMONDBACKS™

WASHINGTON NATIONALS™

BOSTON RED SOX™

DETROIT TIGERS™

HOUSTON ASTROS™

COLLEGIATE COLLECTION

LOYALTY | ENTHUSIASM | PRIDE

Unforgettable memories are made here. Lifelong friendships are created here. Your school is the foundation that will open your mind up to opportunities that will positively change your life. Proudly support the place that will remain forever in your heart.

BOSTON COLLEGE ®

RHODE ISLAND COLLEGE ®

BRYANT UNIVERSITY ®

LOUISIANA STATE UNIVERSITY®

TEXAS A&M UNIVERSITY ®

BOSTON UNIVERSITY ®

UNIVERSITY OF TEXAS ®

PROVIDENCE COLLEGE ®

UNIVERSITY OF CONNECTICUT ®

UNIVERSITY OF NOTRE DAME ®

UNIVERSITY OF SOUTH CAROLINA®

UNIVERSITY OF CONNECTICUT ®

BRYANT UNIVERSITY ®

UNIVERSITY OF RHODE ISLAND®

VANDERBILT UNIVERSITY ®

UNIVERSITY OF ALABAMA®

SORORITY COLLECTION

SISTERHOOD | TRADITION | LOYALTY

Woman are bonded in the deep, mysterious ways of nature. Intuitive and open hearted, they keep the Earthly balance that comes with consistently nurturing loved ones. Committed to tradition and upholding the spirit of philanthropy, sorority sisters are lifelong friends that ignite positive change.

DELTA GAMMA

ALPHA CHI OMEGA

GAMMA PHI BETA

ALPHA PHI

DELTA DELTA DELTA

DELTA ZETA

KAPPA ALPHA THETA

ALPHA SIGMA ALPHA

ALPHA SIGMA TAU

ALPHA OMICRON PI

KAPPA DELTA

CHI OMEGA

DELTA PHI EPSILON

ALPHA GAMMA DELTA

KAPPA KAPPA GAMMA

ALPHA EPSILON PHI

ALPHA DELTA PI

ALPHA XI DELTA

PHI MU

| LICENSED PRODUCTS |

PHI SIGMA SIGMA

THETA PHI ALPHA

SIGMA DELTA TAU

SIGMA SIGMA SIGMA

PI BETA PHI

ZETA TAU ALPHA

SIGMA KAPPA

ARMY

LOYALTY | STRENGTH | RESPECT

The embodiment of physical strength, emotional strength, and strength of purpose, the United States Army creates heroes. Ready to serve our country in any way at any moment, the Army is a patriotic community built on loyalty and respect. A symbol of endurance and skill, channel the energy of the Army Charm to stay strong in all endeavors.

NAVY

DEDICATION | PROTECTION COURAGE

A global force for good, the United States Navy serves as an essential force of stability in our interconnected world. With extraordinary people, leading technology, and incredible capabilities, the Navy positively impacts the globe. Embrace the valiant energy of the Navy Charm as a source of protection, pride, and honor.

MARINES

PRIDE | COMMITMENT | HONOR

A with a strong commitment to develop quality citizens and defend our country at all costs, the Marines are a tight-knit force. Protecting our nation at home and our interests abroad, the Marines base their steadfast values on their motto, Semper Fidelis, meaning, "always faithful." Channel the enduring commitment and strength of the Marines Charm as a proud symbol of patriotism.

COAST GUARD

HONOR | RESPECT | DEVOTION

Built on loyal teamwork and devoted preparation, the Coast Guard protects American shores and citizens around the world. To be always ready is the promise the Coast Guard has made to the nation, to stay ready is the promise the service and its members have made to one another. Embrace the courageous energy of the Unites States Coast Guard Charm as a tribute to this patriotic, honorable force.

AIR FORCE

INTEGRITY | EXCELLENCE SERVICE

With three imperative core values of integrity first, service before self, and excellence in all actions, the Air Force symbolizes courage. The Air Force has a global vision to protect our country and our citizens across the world in all airspaces. Embrace the brave, adventurous energy of the Air Force Charm as a loyal testament to the men and women who keep our skies safe.

By federal law, licensing fees paid to the U.S. Army for the use of its trademarks provide support to the Army Trademark Licensing Program, and net licensing revenue is devoted to U.S. Army Morale, Welfare, and Recreation programs.

Alex and Ani | 105

| LICENSED PRODUCTS |

OLYMPIC COLLECTION

TEAM USA SHIELD

*PROTECTION | COURAGE
VICTORY*

A symbol of strength, the shield is a guiding force meant to protect the wearer in all endeavors. Inspiring achievement, the Olympic Games open us up to the possibilities in persistence. Encouraging the wearer to live stronger and reach higher, adorn yourself with the Team USA Shield Charm for all the courage to overcome all obstacles.

TEAM USA

*PRIDE | DETERMINATION
VICTORY*

A mix of willpower and strength, the energy of the Olympic Games is competitive, determined, and heartfelt. Inspiring achievement, the Olympic Games open us up to possibilities in persistence. Encouraging the wearer to reach higher, live stronger, and love greater, adorn yourself with the Team USA Charm as a symbol of America's extraordinary patriotism.

USA OLYMPIC CHARM

PRIDE | FREEDOM | VICTORY

Symbolizing loyalty, dedication, and the freedom to pursue greatness, the Official USA Olympic Charm recognizes America's extraordinary patriotism. The stars and stripes mixed with the unifying rings encourage us to reach higher, live stronger, and love greater. Wear the Official USA Olympic Charm to inspire achievement, accept leadership, and embrace possibilities.

*PRIDE | DETERMINATION
VICTORY*

A mix of willpower and strength, the energy of the Olympic Games is competitive, determined, and heartfelt. Inspiring achievement, the Olympic Games open us up to possibilities in persistence. Encouraging the wearer to reach higher, live stronger, and love greater, adorn yourself with the Olympic Collection as a symbol of America's extraordinary patriotism.

USA FIVE RING - BLUE

USA FIVE RING - GOLD

USA FIVE RING - WHITE

USA FIVE RING - RED

TOWER BRIDGE

*TRANSITION | CONFIDENCE
POSSIBILITY*

A historic symbol of London, the Tower Bridge stands proudly over the River Thames. This iconic bridge represents movement, transition, and an individual's journey. Adorn yourself with the Tower Bridge Charm as a reminder to consistently move forward and cross into the future with your head held high.

APHRODITE

BEAUTY | CHARM | INSPIRATION

Representing the divine feminine that inspires passionate love, Aphrodite is the goddess of beauty, love, and desire. Birthed from the sea foam, she is usually depicted standing in a seashell. Embrace the irresistible force of Aphrodite's essence in order to strengthen unions and ignite your passions.

ARTEMIS

*HUNTRESS | -ECO-
CONSCIOUSNESS | WILD*

Depicted carrying a bow and arrow, Artemis is the goddess of the wilderness, animals, and fertility. The twin sister of Apollo, Artemis is a strong feminine figure who is always willing to fight for other creatures. Allow the spirited energy of Artemis into your soul as a source of protection and bravery.

HERMES

*DEPENDABLE | HUMOROUS
DIPLOMATIC*

The great communicator and trusted messenger of the gods, Hermes is a respected muse who provides great thought, inspiration, and important guidance from the spirit. The god of travel and diplomacy, he is a well-known trickster yet a loyal companion. Call on Hermes if you have a message to be heard and when you are ready to embrace adventure and new beginnings.

| LICENSED PRODUCTS |

POSEIDON

PROTECTION | INNOVATION
NAVIGATION

The guardian of the sea, floods, and earthquakes, Poseidon represents the mystery of the ocean and the treasures that lie within. Known as the "Earth Shaker," fishermen have shrines of Poseidon for protection. Channel Poseidon's energy to navigate life's journey precisely and to shake things up when necessary.

ZEUS

STRENGTH | LEADERSHIP
COURAGE

The great father and king of all Olympian gods and goddesses, Zeus ruled over the sky, weather, order, and fate. Known to carry the royal scepter, Zeus is usually depicted with a lightening bolt signifying environmental control and absolute power. Connect with the energy of Zeus for divine guidance and the intellectual courage to take action.

APOLLO

SUNLIGHT | CREATIVITY
HEALING

Associated with truth, light, healing, and music, Apollo is the vibrant god of the sun. Apollo's light nourishes all life on Earth and provides the wearer with artistic insight and a sunny disposition. Embrace Apollo's energy for mental, physical, and soulful healing that will lead to creative inspiration and spiritual enlightenment.

ATHENA

INTELLIGENT | CREATIVE
REVOLUTIONARY

Goddess of wisdom, inspiration, and the arts, Athena represents the knowledgeable aspects of the divine feminine. Protector of the written word and capable of great inventions, she is a reminder to fearlessly open your imagination. Embrace the energy of Athena for revolutionary ideas, intellectual insight, and artistic power.

KENTUCKY DERBY™ 138 HORSE

ENERGY | POWER | PASSION

Giving us the strength to move forward towards our dreams, the Kentucky Derby™ 138 Horse Charm evokes the passion and diligence necessary to triumph. With deep roots and a zealous following, the Kentucky Derby™ is a symbol of freedom. Embrace the energy of the Kentucky Derby™ 138 Horse Charm for the power to ride the wind and embrace your possibilities.

ICONIC HORSESHOE

SUCCESS | TRADITION | VICTORY

Every year the victor of the Kentucky Derby™ is taken to the winner's circle and adorned in a garland of red roses. Originally a gift for the ladies of the Derby, the roses symbolize the heart of a winner and the grand spirit of the race. An emblem of success, the Iconic Horseshoe Charm is a reminder that perseverance and great faith will lead to victory.

HORSE SADDLE

GRACE | POWER | FREEDOM

Encouraging collaboration, a saddle brings a horse and human together to harness their power in order to explore. The saddle allows an individual to take charge and to ride the winds of possibility. Adorn yourself with the Horse Saddle Charm to gear up for the adventures in life and to lovingly pay tribute to the loyal animals that can take you there.

DECORATIVE HAT

PRIDE | TRADITION | DISTINCTION

A social accessory traditionally worn at female gatherings, the decorative hat represents an individual looking and being at one's best Distinctively adorned hats are bold pieces that symbolize an outgoing nature and a proud heart. Channel the energy of the Decorative Hat Charm as a symbol of empowerment.

MINT JULEP

CAREFREE | TRADITION
CELEBRATION

A traditional beverage from the south, the mint julep puts an emphasis on flavor, aroma, and carefree living. The mint julep is an iconic part of spectator horse races, with over 120,000 being sold annually during the early spring. A reminder that joyful spirits and festivities are good for the soul, adorn yourself with the Mint Julep Charm to celebrate vivaciousness.

WORDS ARE POWERFUL - CAROLYN RAFAELIAN

"Words are Powerful." What does that mean? What a world we'd live in if people could fully understand how powerful their thoughts and words are. In these modern times, though we are supposed to be more enlightened, we've lost a lot of the organic ability to communicate, not with technology, but with our own inherent resources. Strip us of cell phones, computers, everything, and how do you live? Who do you communicate with? You still have your thoughts, you still have a divine way, and you still have what some might call free will, but what you really have is your own perspective.

You can take one situation and put ten people in it, and every one of them will emerge with a different result. Some will make the situation worse, some will make it better – it's really based on the particular individual's synergy with that incident. What many people don't realize is how powerful they are – that they have the gift to create their own perspective in any situation; it's all in how they choose to use it.

So, there are some people who will always make matters worse, because if you're constantly thinking of negative things, that's what you manifest. But if you wake up every day, even if your situation's not where you need it to be, and you don't dwell on it, but instead say, "Today I'm going to make moves to make things better" then that's

what you manifest as well. You have the power, through your thoughts, to identify that this isn't OK or enough for me and by doing so you invite anything that wants to come in your life and bring a different outlook. Powerful.

Your words are physical manifestations of your thoughts. So, for example, when you're thinking of the word "love," it's an energy, and it spreads. It's love – it has its own vibe, and it goes. Alternatively, even ugly words, like "liar," invoke a feeling, a vibe, and when you call someone these things, you're attaching that energy to that person. And in return, that energy gets bounced back to you. Words are powerful.

When you realize words are powerful, you embolden yourself to take control of your words and the way they impact others. So if you say something hurtful, you can say, "You know what? I didn't mean that. I take it back." And you cancel it out. And then you become more comfortable in yourself and realize it's OK to make mistakes and say, "I was out of line." The goal is that you get to be so comfortable in your own skin that things aren't so fearful anymore, and you're doing it for the right reasons. Not for external reasons, like what people would think of you. You're doing it because it feels right to you."

PHOTO CREDITS:

ALL INTERVIEW PORTRAITS WERE TAKEN BY CYD MCKENNA WITH THE EXCEPTION OF:

P. 17: BABIES BY ROSIE MCGOWAN

P. 60: ADAM AND CASEY WOOD BY RHYANNE KETRON

ALL BANGLE SHOTS BY JOHN SMITH, III AND CYD MCKENNA

ADDITIONAL PHOTO CREDITS:

P. 8: CAROLYN AT THE DEAD SEA, BY DAVID BETTENCOURT

P. 10: CAROLYN AT THE CHURCH OF THE SEPULCHRE BY DAVID BETTENCOURT

P.18: RAFAELIAN FAMILY ARCHIVE

P. 25: RAFAELIAN FAMILY ARCHIVE

P. 26: CINERAMA EXTERIOR BY DAVID BETTENCOURT

P. 28: CAROLYN AND RALPH RAFAELIAN, BY SANDOR BODO, COURTESY OF THE PROVIDENCE JOURNAL

P 31: RAFAELIAN FAMILY ARCHIVES

P. 41: POSITIVE ENERGY SUNSHINE BY CYD MCKENNA

P. 46: FAMILY PHOTOGRAPH, BY KERRY PERDOSO

ALL FACTORY SHOTS BY CYD MCKENNA

P. 62: CAROLYN RAFAELIAN BY DAVID BETTENCOURT

P. 67: DAVID BETTENCOURT

P. 68: CYD MCKENNA

P. 76: CAROLYN RAFAELAIN AND NICKY CASTONGUAY-MAHER BY DAVID BETTENCOURT

BIOGRAPHY PICTURE OF GIOVANNI FEROCE BY DAVID BETTENCOURT

BIOGRAPHY PICTURE OF CYD MCKENNA BY EOIN MCKENNA